THE BASIS OF
RELIGIOUS
LIBERTY

THE BASIS OF
RELIGIOUS
LIBERTY

*

A. F. CARRILLO DE ALBORNOZ

*Secretariat for Religious Liberty,
World Council of Churches*

ASSOCIATION PRESS
NEW YORK 7, N.Y.

CONTENTS

APPENDICES

PREFACE

THE MAIN aim of this study is to stimulate discussion within the World Council of Churches and the Churches themselves on problems of religious liberty.

For more than three years, the Secretariat for Religious Liberty and its Commission have been trying to find 'a solidly established basis for our Christian attitude concerning religious freedom', as was asked of them by the Central Committee at Nyborg, 1958.

The results of this study have been useful, but so far are known only to a limited number of specialists and theologians. Now the time has come for churches and Christian people more generally to enter into discussion about a matter in which they are passionately interested. In view of these circumstances, the Third Assembly of the World Council of Churches, New Delhi, November–December, 1961, decided 'that the Committee and Secretariat [for Religious Liberty] arrange for the publication of a brochure or booklet, based principally on studies done by the Commission and Secretariat up to this time, for the use of the churches and regional councils. This publication should seek to state clearly the issues that have arisen during the discussions, as well as the points on which significant agreement has been reached. It should include pertinent questions and be suitable for use as the basis of discussion in different parts of the world.'[1]

We think that all the important issues concerning religious liberty and discussed in our Commission could be grouped under these main subjects:

(a) the nature of religious liberty, or what is religious freedom;
(b) the basis of religious liberty, or investigation of the grounds on which we claim religious liberty; and
(c) the conditions for securing religious liberty in the world, or how religious freedom can be practically recognized and exercised according to different circumstances.

As this book is addressed to Christian people generally, its

[1] *The New Delhi Report. The Third Assembly of the World Council of Churches* 1961, p. 168.

characteristics should be clarity and simplicity. This is not an easy task, for various questions involved are of particular theological difficulty. Nevertheless, we have tried to say things as simply as possible.

One of our main difficulties is precisely that for saying 'things' we must employ 'terms'; and terminology on religious liberty has lately become rather complicated. In our opinion, discussions on terminology should be avoided here. We will therefore try to explain clearly the thing itself designated by each term, and the sense in which the terms are used, without pressing the adoption of the terms themselves but leaving to others the liberty to use these terms otherwise.

Readers will frequently find citations of ecumenical statements on religious freedom. Ecumenical statements are not cited here as a final and authoritative response to the questions discussed. Ecumenical statements are not infallible. They surely are subject to revision. Nevertheless, when they particularly reflect a considerable degree of ecumenical unanimity, they may and should constitute a useful light for orientating our investigation and they should not be rejected without mature reflection and study.

Three final observations should still be made in this preface:

Readers should not expect to find here all the possible questions concerning religious liberty; we have limited ourselves to those discussed by the Commission which we nevertheless think to be the most important ones.

Secondly, while this book could not have been written without the outstanding co-operation of many specialists who intervened in past discussions, nevertheless the opinions expressed in it do not engage the responsibility of the Secretariat for Religious Liberty, still less that of the World Council of Churches, but exclusively reflect the personal thinking of the author.

Lastly, there is almost no reference to bibliography, for this study does not reflect the literature on religious liberty but the discussions held within our own Commission and the study groups.

A. F. CARRILLO DE ALBORNOZ

INTRODUCTION

RELIGIOUS freedom is an ecumenical question of primary importance in itself and specially in the world today. As the General Secretary said at Rolle, 'it ought to be unnecessary to underline that the World Council intends to continue the struggle for religious liberty, for we have given sufficient proofs that we consider such liberty essential for the sake of the Christian witness' (*Minutes and Reports of the Fourth Meeting of the Central Committee, Rolle, August 1951*, p. 62). The WCC is fully entitled to protect and promote religious liberty. Moreover, it is one of the main problems which the WCC has the right and the duty to submit to thorough study. The first practical conclusion to be drawn from this obvious truth is that the WCC should not place this problem on the outer fringe of its main activities, merely dealing with it piecemeal as occasion arises.

The WCC must be absolutely clear about its ultimate aim: '*ut unum sint*'. But the only way to attain this goal is by freedom in charity. The Archbishop of Canterbury has said very rightly: 'That [a united Church] will not come as long as our Christian faith is not strong enough to bear each other's differences and to refuse to reduce them by force.' Intolerance is found in the antipodes of unity and charity. Hence one of the most important aims of the WCC must be to promote universal religious freedom in which alone an atmosphere of unity and love is possible.

However, the ecumenical movement, in caring for religious liberty, not only considers the churches which belong to it, but it has regard for and seeks to serve all Christians, including those who stand outside it, and even all men, non-religious as well as religious ones.

This care for religious freedom is all the more urgent and necessary in that freedoms in general and religious liberty in particular are being abridged in the world today and may continue to be so. Therefore, it is our duty as Christians and as men to claim and to defend this fundamental liberty.

Our first and foremost problem is to investigate what we

Christians think about religious liberty and what reasons in a Christian perspective we have to proclaim and to seek it.

Emphasis should be laid on the unique importance of this undertaking as an attempt to provide a thorough and deep-going study with sound theological grounding. In their responses to Evanston, several member churches asked what the specific Christian contribution should be in matters of religious liberty. Particularly, they would like to have a clearer definition of the relation between such standards as embodied in the United Nations Charter and the universal Declaration of Human Rights and the specific theological approach which sees the dignity of man in the light of God's ultimate design.[1]

This need of emphasis on the theological point has been confirmed by a distinguished layman, Dr Charles Malik (former Chairman of the U.N. Commission on Human Rights):

> 'The crisis of human rights consists precisely in the fact that politics is meddling in a field that belongs more properly to the moral and prophetic consciousness. Politics should follow; it should not lead. When, contrary to nature, it is leading in these fundamental matters, then there is something the matter with the Church. For I do not believe the Church . . . is leading enough in this field.'[2]

To no other human right and to no other world problem better than to the problem of religious liberty apply these words of Dr Fagley (Executive Secretary of the C.C.I.A.):

> 'A recognized major weakness of the past decade is the insufficient attention given to the underlying theological presuppositions of ecumenical action in world affairs. . . . The need for thorough study on the relation of the Christian faith to the principles of world community advanced on behalf of the churches is urgent.'[3]

Our study should therefore ask 'whether there are specifically theological grounds which supply a content to the conception of religious liberty and justify claims on its behalf'.[4]

Of course, there are already some insights concerning religious liberty which are unanimously accepted among the member churches. Particularly:

[1] *Response to Evanston*, Geneva, 1957, p. 39.
[2] *The Ecumenical Review*, vol. VIII, No. 4, July, 1956, pp. 408–409.
[3] 'Christian Witness in the World of Nations', *The Ecumenical Review*, vol. VIII, No. 4, p. 392.
[4] Central Committee of the World Council of Churches, Nyborg, 1958, *Minutes*, p. 84.

(*a*) On the level of general Christian convictions, it seems to be solidly established that the member churches consider religious liberty as a part of their religious insights.

(*b*) On the level of ecumenical strategy, they think religious liberty to be a necessary climate and atmosphere in which the ecumenical dialogue can flourish.

(*c*) Finally, well aware of the fundamental missionary task of the Church, they do not hesitate to claim religious liberty to proclaim Christ's Message everywhere in the world.

Nevertheless, a deep-going theological study encounters certain difficulties which we would like to explain here.

First of all, to have a *Christian* idea of religious freedom and a *Christian* basis for it necessitates some theological reflection which only theologians can do. On the other hand, *social* and *external* religious liberty is not, *in itself*, a theological concept. It belongs rather to sociology and law. No wonder then that theologians are somewhat uneasy when they come to investigate it. Furthermore, theologians used to have theological traditions, some of them centuries old, which are precious in some dogmatic respects but which are sometimes rather cumbersome for the understanding of a concept of social religious freedom which is very modern indeed. To give only one example of this: we would like to remind everyone that the traditional body of theological thought, both Roman Catholic and Protestant, was developed at a time when the principle of coercive authority, whether in the Church or in the State, was completely in the ascendant and scarcely open to challenge. We now live in an age in which co-operation is replacing coercion as the normative principle of human relations. This requires some re-thinking of the ethical Christian doctrine.

Another difficulty (or rather, a series of difficulties) originates in what could be called 'the apologetic complex'.

It is obvious that religious liberty is largely violated in many countries and even its principles are often denied by various forms of modern thought. In view of these facts, it is only natural that Christians approach the problems of religious freedom with 'apologetic' feelings.

What happens to Christians generally happens in particular to the World Council of Churches. On the level of 'policy', the WCC has to make statements and to take remedial measures against infractions of religious liberty. On this level, and in regard to factual situations, it is very difficult to avoid the apologetic attitude, but probably it is the only one to be taken.

When it comes to making statements of principle, the WCC is also biased by events. The statements, even the doctrinal ones, are often urged and occasioned by the knowledge of the facts of particular situations and by the contrast, in some cases very sharp, between the world situation and our ecumenical feelings and insights concerning religious freedom. Therefore, it is not surprising that some statements of principle show a somewhat 'apologetic' tendency and seem to be 'fighting' the enemies of religious liberty, be they the State, other churches or society in general.

Nevertheless, although recognizing the practical justification of this attitude, the apologetic point of view is not the most correct and useful one, at least in doctrinal investigation. For the sake of religious freedom itself, we have tried to avoid this 'apologetic' bias, and to explain our Christian convictions as objectively as possible.

I

WHAT IS RELIGIOUS LIBERTY?

I

WHAT KIND OF RELIGIOUS LIBERTY DO ECUMENICAL BODIES CLAIM?

THE TERM 'religious liberty' is a most vague one and it is used for designating many different kinds of religious freedom. The subject of our study being precisely the kind of religious liberty *which the ecumenical bodies claim* in their declarations and statements, our first task is to identify it clearly and to distinguish it from any other kind of religious freedom.

Ecumenical statements seldom attempt to define or to describe the kind of religious liberty they are asking for. Nevertheless, we can easily identify, in the same statements, the essential elements of this kind of religious liberty:

(a) The *active subject*, whose faculty it is to exercise religious liberty within society, is the whole human race, every human being, considered on the individual and collective as well as on the corporate and institutional level, and without any limitation with regard to nation, colour, sex, religion, etc.

(b) The *passive subject*, whose duty it is to respect religious liberty of others, is again the human being, every human person, physical or moral, also associations and corporations, also churches or religious bodies and States. In other words, the passive subject is human society in general, including every human being which is external to the active subject.

As a consequence of this:

(1) *It is only the human race*, the human society, individually and collectively, which has the duty to respect this kind of religious freedom; not God. If man enjoys some freedom before God (psychologically, physically or otherwise), this is not the kind of freedom which we study here.

(2) Similarly, it is *the other men* who must respect my religious freedom. For this freedom is essentially social and demands 'alterity' as well as all the other human rights. Therefore, the freedom which I may have before myself or within myself

(which is generally called 'inner' freedom) is not the kind of religious liberty claimed by ecumenical bodies.

(3) Consequently, this freedom being a *social* right, to be respected by the human society, we deem it correct to term it *'social* religious liberty'.

(c) Religious liberty, thus understood, must liberate *from social coercion*.[1] Therefore, social religious liberty does not only exclude juridical or physical compulsion but all the other possible, even often unconscious, coercions coming from society, economic, moral, psychological, etc.

(d) Finally, *the matters* to be protected by this kind of religious liberty are *matters of religion* generally. Here again ecumenical bodies do not make precise what exactly are 'matters of religion', still less what is 'religion'. This is, indeed, a grave question which we should study later. Nevertheless, for the simple purpose of *identification* it is enough to register that in ecumenical statements religious matters include not only the exercise of one's own chosen religion or the right to change one's religion or belief, but also all external activities of worship, preaching, teaching, practice and observance, and even the manifestation in words and deeds of the implications of one's own religious convictions for political, economic or social relations.

In view of this analysis of the ecumenical statements we think we can correctly *identify* (not define) the kind of religious liberty demanded by ecumenical bodies as *the social faculty of every adult human being (individually, collectively or corporately) to be free from social coercion in religious matters.*

Once we have identified the kind of religious liberty which ecumenical bodies demand, we can attempt to distinguish it from other kinds of liberty.

1. In contrast to this social freedom which is immunity or exemption from external coercion, we find the natural *freedom of choice*, which is proper to intellectual creatures and which in itself is independent of, and can co-exist with external compulsion or negation of social liberty. This freedom of choice is often called *internal* liberty in the sense of liberation from internal compulsion, not from social coercion. We have also called this freedom of volition *natural*, not with the intention of opposing it to the *'libertas christiana'* but merely in the sense of a concept which does not include any religious or theological element and which is

---

[1] By the word 'coercion' we understand physical or moral constraint which undermines the ultimate freedom of choice. On the legitimate social influence which is compatible with religious freedom, see Part III, ch. 2, p. 111 ff.

accepted by psychologists of other creeds or philosophical background. It is obvious that our religious liberty and this freedom of volition are different things, for one is external, i.e. liberation from external coercion, while the other is internal, i.e. an exemption from internal compulsion.

2. Several theologians, during our discussions, stressed the fundamental difference between social religious liberty and the '*libertas christiana*', or specific Christian liberty. From the very first mention of the concept of Christian liberty (particularly as proclaimed by the churches of the Reformation) it is evident that this is not the same thing as social external religious liberty. Although ecumenical statements are extremely short of theological distinctions in this matter, the Amsterdam (1948) Declaration on Religious Liberty explicitly distinguishes between 'the liberty with which Christ has set us free', which is 'inner freedom', and 'its outward expression', so that 'all men should have freedom in religious life'.

We think that there is ecumenical agreement on this distinction. It seems plainly evident that social freedom to take and to actualize religious decisions free from social coercion is not the same thing as internal freedom in Christ. The main proof is that they can exist *separately*, as we see in the Christian martyrs.

Where opinions begin to vary is when the question arises of asking how great the differences are between these liberties. For some, they are *entirely* different, so that it would be impossible to establish interrelations between them both, still less to claim the one on grounds of the other. We intend to study this problem deeply in our Part II.

On the other hand, other theologians are not so convinced of the absoluteness of this distinction and wonder whether traditional theology did not make these two liberties seem more different than they are; in other words, whether their interrelations have not been neglected. This is a very interesting and provocative suggestion. Are the two freedoms in part different and in part similar? Considering that the difference clearly consists of the one being external and the other internal, in what way could they be similar? How far and by what wrong arguments or conceptions could traditional theology have represented two freedoms as being more different than they are in reality? We wonder whether we could find the answer to these questions in the following considerations:

(*a*) Has not traditional theology committed the mistake of practising some kind of 'dichotomy of man', considering the *individual* and the *social* being separately, while in fact they are the same thing? Conceptually, we are able to consider internal individual liberty without considering social liberty. But are both liberties so separated in the unique human reality, and even in the freedom in Christ? It would seem, on the contrary, that Christ has set men free precisely in the social context. It is true that we can find both liberties separated, but it is always an unnatural and forced situation: man remains internally free *in spite of* external coercion. We should never neglect the import of this '*in spite of*'.

(*b*) Has not traditional theology emphasized the *objective* aspect of religion too much, and unduly neglected the *subjective* aspect of religious life and its social consequences?

(*c*) Has not traditional theology excessively stressed the importance of 'authority' and of due obedience to Church and State, thus neglecting the necessary social consequences of internal freedom?

It is difficult to give a final response to these questions, since there is no agreement among our theologians on this. But the matter requires elucidation, and churches are called to discuss it.

3. There are still two other terms which we often find, particularly in the literature of the nineteenth century, namely those of 'freedom of worship' and 'freedom of conscience'. In many cases, both expressions have been employed as synonyms for social religious liberty. We think 'freedom of worship' is a very incomplete expression, for the area of social religious freedom is much larger than 'worship'.

Much more difficult is the problem posed by the term 'freedom of conscience'. First of all, it seems that this term, applied to social religious liberty, would solely concern the individual, who alone has 'conscience'. We cannot see how the corporate freedom of the Church, for instance, could be called 'freedom of conscience'. Furthermore the freedom of expression and manifestation of religious beliefs could be understood as 'freedom of conscience' only in an analogical and derivative manner. Therefore, we are reluctant to consider this term as synonymous with 'religious freedom'. Probably 'freedom of conscience' should be accepted as *a part* of social religious liberty in general, and be a matter for study in the following chapter.

We cannot close this chapter without asking ourselves an important question. Does the concept of social religious liberty, as we have identified it in the ecumenical statements, have origin in Christian insights?

To answer this question properly a fundamental distinction is necessary:

(*a*) Certainly *the social religious liberty* demanded by the ecumenical bodies is not in itself, or objectively, a *Christian* liberty, neither the '*libertas christiana*' of the Reformed Tradition, nor any other kind of specific Christian freedom. The plain proof for this is the fact that many non-Christians demand exactly the same social religious freedom that we demand. This is why the World Council of Churches recognizes the correctness of the *area* or *contents* (provided that they are properly interpreted) of religious liberty proclaimed by the Universal Declaration of Human Rights, although the United Nations has not our Christian motivations.[1]

(*b*) Nevertheless, *our own concept* of social religious liberty is Christian. We mean by this that the articulation of its elements and motivations are grounded on our Christian convictions. Thus, we claim religious liberty for *all men* without distinction or discrimination, *for* we believe in the fundamental unity of the human family. We demand protection against every social coercion, *for* we believe that even the State must respect man's highest loyalties. We ask for liberty in a very large area of religious activities, even for the proclamation of the political and social implications of our religious beliefs, *in virtue of* our Christian understanding of religion. Of course, we have said that many non-Christians demand exactly the same social religious liberty as we. But, on the other hand, many other non-Christians have other very different concepts of religious liberty, precisely on the ground of their different religious or philosophical insights, as we shall see later. In this sense we may say correctly that *our own notion* of social religious liberty is fully Christian.

[1] *Article 18* of the 'Universal Declaration of Human Rights' adopted by the General Assembly of the United Nations on December 10, 1948: 'Everyone has the right to freedom of thought, conscience and religion; this right includes freedom to change his religion or belief, and freedom, either alone or in community with others and in public or private, to manifest his religion or belief in teaching, practice, worship and observance.'

2

RELIGIOUS LIBERTY & THE VARIOUS RELIGIOUS FREEDOMS IN ECUMENICAL THINKING

READING THE various ecumenical statements and ecumenical literature generally, we must agree on the fact that sometimes social religious liberty, as we identified it in the previous chapter, is mentioned *in the singular* and considered as a whole; while, on other occasions, there appear *many religious freedoms*, very different from each other in specification and in object, although all correspond to the general concept of external and social religious liberty.

We therefore consider it necessary to investigate the sense given by ecumenical statements to the general concept of 'religious liberty' in the singular; the significations of the various 'religious liberties'; and finally, the interrelations and eventual differences among the various religious freedoms with and from each other and their 'genus'.

Concerning the general concept of 'religious liberty', in the singular, the ecumenical statements do not give us a definition of it, but we can find in them some significant elements of a description.

Thus, for instance, in some cases negative formulations are employed, as very recently in the Declaration on Religious Liberty by the Third Assembly of the World Council of Churches, New Delhi, 1961, where it is said that 'human attempts by legal enactment or by pressure of social custom to coerce or to eliminate faith' constitute a violation of religious liberty.

On other occasions, religious liberty is positively described as 'the social possibility of acting responsibly in matters of religion'.[1]

---

[1] First Assembly of the WCC, Amsterdam, 1948, Report on 'The Church and the Disorder of Society'. Cf. the formulation of the Declaration by the New Delhi Assembly: 'That every person has opportunity for the responsible exercise' of religious liberty.

Putting together the negative and the positive elements of these descriptions, we could formulate social religious liberty in general as the right of every human being to be free from social or legal coercion in religious matters, as well as man's responsibility to secure that all possess this freedom. Perhaps the most complete formulation is that of the 'Christian Statement' submitted by the Commission on Religious Liberty to the Central Committee at St Andrews, 1960, which reads:

> *The faculty of every human being, individually or in corporate bodies, publicly or in private, to be free from social or legal coercion in religious matters, and to be free for the proclamation of his faith, and the expression of its implications among his fellow men.*[1]

Now what is the content of the various 'religious freedoms' so often related in ecumenical documents?

Sometimes ecumenical bodies have made no attempt to make systematic classifications of the various religious freedoms but merely give a list, more or less complete, of such freedoms. For instance:

> 'We affirm the primary right to religious worship, and the converse right to refuse compliance with any form of worship unacceptable on grounds of conscience. We affirm the right to public witness to religion, and the right to religious teaching, especially in the nurture of the young.'[2]

> 'The right of individuals everywhere to religious liberty shall be recognized. . . . Religious liberty shall be interpreted to include freedom to worship according to conscience and to bring up children in the faith of their parents; freedom for the individual to change his religion; freedom to preach, educate, publish, and carry on missionary activities; and freedom to organise with others, and to acquire and hold property, for these purposes.'[3]

The impression one gets from these enumerations and other similar ones,[4] is that the liberties cited are indeed very different and that perhaps they are not exactly of the same nature, nor should they be regulated by the same principles.

---

[1] Copies available at the secretariat for Religious Liberty. Some consider the word 'faculty' outmoded. It may be so, and we would be grateful for the suggestion of another more modern. What the Commission wished to mean by this word is that religious liberty is not merely *a legal right*, but also a general human faculty to be respected by society even outside legal provisions or state protection.

[2] The World Conference on Church, Community and State, Oxford, 1937.

[3] The Federal Council of the Churches of Christ in America, 1944.

[4] Cf. also Conference on the World Mission of the Church, Madras, 1938.

Fortunately, twice we find among these enumerations an attempt at classification, which will be useful for our purpose.

The Declaration on Religious Liberty made by the Amsterdam Assembly (1948) classifies the long list of liberties into four main groups, which it formulates as follows:

(a) 'Every person has the right to determine his own faith and creed.'
(b) 'Every person has the right to express his religious beliefs in worship, teaching and practice, and to proclaim the implications of his beliefs for relationships in a social or political community.'
(c) 'Every person has the right to associate with others and to organise with them for religious purposes.'
(d) 'Every religious organisation, formed or maintained by action in accordance with the rights of individual persons, has the right to determine its policies and practices for the accomplishment of its chosen purposes.'[1]

Similarly, the Conference of the Protestant Latin European Churches distinguished three groups of religious freedoms:

(a) 'Individual freedom';
(b) 'collective freedom'; and
(c) 'institutional and corporate freedoms.'[2]

These two classifications complete each other. The (b) of the second, 'collective freedom', obviously corresponds to the (c) of the first or the right to associate and organize with others, although we would prefer the expression 'freedom of religious association'. Similarly, the (c) of the second, 'institutional and corporate freedom', corresponds to the (d) of the first, on the rights and liberties of religious organizations. The only substantial difference is that the Amsterdam Assembly distinguishes two kinds of 'individual freedoms', namely 'the right to determine his own faith and creed' and 'the right to express his religious beliefs'.

Thus we would have four main groups of religious freedoms:

Liberty of conscience, or right to determine freely his own faith and creed;
Liberty of religious expression;
Liberty of religious association; and
Corporate and institutional religious freedom.

We have called the right to determine freely his own faith and creed, *liberty of conscience*. Indeed, we think that this expression

[1] First Assembly of the WCC, Amsterdam, 1948, Declaration on Religious Liberty.
[2] Conference of the Protestant Churches of the Latin European Countries, Chambon-sur-Lignon, France, 1958, Resolutions on Religious Liberty.

corresponds more exactly to this particular freedom, rather than to religious liberty in general, for liberty of conscience means primarily the faculty of taking internal religious decisions, free from every social or external compulsion. Note that we do not identify 'liberty of conscience' with *inner* liberty. For us, liberty of conscience is that kind of *external* or social religious freedom which gives us the possibility of making personal judgments and decisions concerning our own religious beliefs without any social coercion. Besides, the Amsterdam Declaration also considers this liberty of conscience as an external freedom, for it states, in its own context, that 'religious, social and political institutions have the obligation to permit the mature individual to relate himself to sources of information in such a way as to allow personal religious decision and belief'.[1] We underline this because sometimes, during our discussions, some confusion arose in this respect, probably on the grounds that the *activity* protected by the liberty of conscience is mostly internal, while the essential element of freedom, which is *liberation from*, is always external, i.e. liberation from external or social compulsion.

We are satisfied that these four kinds of religious freedoms, liberty of conscience, liberty of religious expression, liberty of religious association and institutional and corporate freedom, include all possible social religious freedoms and that, therefore, this classification is complete and adequate.[2]

We should now investigate whether these four kinds of religious freedoms are of the same 'species' or, on the contrary, whether there are specific differences between them. This we can ascertain only by investigating the very nature of each.

As for the first, freedom of conscience or freedom to take religious decisions and to choose freely one's own religion or belief, its elements and the realm of its activities exclusively concern religion in itself. We have already spoken of the difficulty of defining 'religion'. Nevertheless, and without entering into deep theological studies, it seems evident that religion refers at least to the personal and essential relation of man to God, as

---

[1] First Assembly of the WCC, Amsterdam, 1948, Declaration on Religious Liberty.
[2] Note that religious liberty of the family and for educating children is included, partly in the liberty of conscience, partly in the liberty of religious expression.

Creator, Redeemer and Sanctifier. Religion consists substantially in this fundamental dependence of man, so fundamental that, *for this purpose*, it makes man independent from everything and everybody besides God. Religious liberty, therefore, *in its essential purity*, is the liberation of man from every social compulsion concerning *his essential relations with God*. Now, it is obvious that the essential relations of man with God are constituted by his faith, by his religious beliefs, by his personal worship, by his acting according to his own religious convictions, i.e. the kind of activities protected by the liberty of conscience.

Different is the case concerning the three other kinds of religious liberty. The *liberty of religious expression* presupposes something more than man's complete dependence on God and his essential relation to him; it also presupposes that man is essentially a social being and that the *expression* of his thoughts and feelings is a fundamental human right. The right of expression, being one of the most fundamental human rights, makes it obvious that the liberty of religious expression must be considered as sacred and therefore recognized and respected by society. Nevertheless, we should not forget that this kind of religious liberty is not exclusively based, as is liberty of conscience, on the essential relations of man with God, but *also* on the general human right of expression. If the nature of the created and redeemed man were not social, we could not speak of liberty of religious expression in spite of man's essential relations with God.

Similarly, the 'liberty of religious association' and the 'corporate and institutional religious freedom' originate from the combination of general human rights of association and corporate freedom with religious liberty itself. In other words, these two kinds of religious liberty presuppose not only religious freedom in itself, but also the recognition of the general human right to associate with others and freely to administer corporations.

Without pressing the adoption of this terminology, but only in the interests of clarity, we would call the freedom of religious expression, the freedom of religious association and the corporate and institutional religious freedom, *mixed religious freedoms*, in the sense that these three types of religious liberty presuppose not only 'pure' religious freedom itself, but also the fundamental human rights of expression, association and of corporate freedom.

There is another sense of the term 'mixed' which we deem very

important. Calling those religious freedoms 'mixed' we would
like to point out that they are not *simply a case*, among others, of
the liberties of expression, association and corporation. Being
'mixed' freedoms, i.e. presupposing as their essential elements
religious liberty in itself *and* the other related freedoms, their
concept and their evaluation will depend *on both* elements involved.
Thus, for instance, the freedom of religious expression must be
studied and estimated not only as a simple case of liberty of
expression, but also as a case of specific religious freedom. Both
elements, both values, as they enter into the composition of the
'mixed' freedom, complete and limit each other mutually.

Summing up in a synoptic way what has been said, we would
have the following descriptive outline:

I. PURE RELIGIOUS LIBERTY (Supreme independence of man's essential relations with God)	= 'LIBERTY OF CONSCIENCE'
II. RELIGIOUS LIBERTY+ HUMAN RIGHT OF EXPRESSION	= 'LIBERTY OF RELIGIOUS EXPRESSION'
III. RELIGIOUS LIBERTY+ HUMAN RIGHT OF ASSOCIATION	= 'LIBERTY OF RELIGIOUS ASSOCIATION'
IV. RELIGIOUS LIBERTY+ HUMAN RIGHT OF CORPORATE FREEDOM	= 'CORPORATE AND INSTITUTIONAL RELIGIOUS FREEDOM'

With this important distinction we believe to have contributed
to the solution of a grave question which has been discussed by
our theologians. Many specialists thought that religious freedom
was 'a supreme value' inasmuch as it protects man's eternal relations
with God. Therefore they were very much reluctant to see the
concept of religious freedom limited by social or legal considerations. On the other hand, many others deemed it impossible and
absurd to leave society unarmed against every possible abuse, even
crimes and murders, committed on pretext of religious convictions. We think that, although 'pure' religious liberty in itself
is a supreme value, nevertheless the 'mixed' religious freedoms
depend also, in their conception and valuation, on the conception
and valuation of the other human rights involved. It would be,
therefore, contrary to reality and to social exigencies to apply
without distinction to these 'mixed' freedoms general principles
exclusively derived from the concept of 'pure' religious liberty.
This consideration will be of paramount importance when we

treat the problems of the responsible exercise of religious freedom.[1]

After these considerations it appears clear that when ecumenical bodies speak generally of 'religious liberty', in the singular, they employ a 'genus' which includes all the four kinds of related freedoms. Following this terminology, when we speak in this study of 'religious liberty', we shall always mean *all* social or external religious freedoms and not only the kind which we called 'pure' or 'liberty of conscience', but also those liberties called 'mixed' or which are constituted by the religious freedom and other elements not specifically religious, as are the rights of expression, association and corporation. Of course, others may use terms otherwise and call 'religious liberty' only that notion which does not presuppose other human rights not specifically religious. Both terminologies are perfectly legitimate. But in the second case, when we speak of 'religious liberty' in the 'pure' sense, or 'liberty of conscience', we may not use the same term as a 'genus' of all kinds of religious freedoms, and still less predicate of each of the 'mixed' freedoms what we said about liberty of conscience. For instance, if we affirm that society may not *in any case* limit our 'pure' religious freedom or our complete autonomy in our essential relations with God, this assertion may not, without distinction, be applied to the mixed freedoms or freedoms of expression, association and corporation.

In discussion about the nature of religious liberty there is often question of problems of conscience, and various and even opposite opinions thereon are expressed. Owing to this and to the general suggestion that these problems of conscience related to religious liberty needed more thorough treatment, we shall discuss this matter in the following chapter.

[1] See below, Part III, ch. 5, p. 135 ff.

3

HOW FAR DO PROBLEMS OF CONSCIENCE ENTER INTO THE CONSIDERATION OF SOCIAL RELIGIOUS FREEDOM?

IT IS almost impossible to speak about religious freedom without mentioning the word 'conscience'. In the liberal individualistic tradition of the nineteenth century, people, even scholars and specialists, did not speak of 'religious liberty', but of 'liberty of conscience'. In our days, many still employ both terms as equivalent.

Furthermore, the word 'conscience' occurs frequently in the definition or description of social or external religious liberty; for instance it is said that religious liberty is 'the right freely to exercise religious activities *according to conscience*'.

Moreover, there is controversy among theologians about what is called the 'absoluteness' or the 'primacy' of conscience. Some believe that the primacy of conscience must be absolutely respected, so that no one has the right to interfere in matters of conscience concerning others, forcing them to act against their conscience or preventing them from doing what their conscience urges them to do. Others, on the contrary, think that these assertions, as they stand, cannot be accepted.

Thus we see that the inclusion of these and other particular problems concerning 'conscience' in the general questions of religious liberty obliges us to investigate some difficult and controversial points:

1. It is very important to determine what exactly this 'primacy' of conscience consists of, and how far it is 'absolute'. For us Christians the only *objectively* absolute thing is the divine revealed truth. A wrong opinion even when it is held in all good conscience is, nevertheless, bad. The judgment of conscience '*in bona fide*' can therefore be absolute only *for the subject* of this judgment, as

far as it is impossible for him otherwise to find the real objective truth or the right moral rule he was looking for. But are church and society obliged to respect the mistaken conscience?

2. This, of course, poses the problem of knowing the extent to which conscience should be enlightened in order that freedom may be exercised. Would it be enough to say that my '*bona fide*' conscience tells me, right or wrong, to have freedom to follow the criterion of my own conscience? For many, theology should differentiate more fully between the image of God as the continuous objective work of God in Revelation, and the conscience as relative, subject to man's training, experience and reasoning, especially perhaps to the pressures of his environment. As said one of our best advisers, 'I should personally stress much more fully the need to subject conscience to the image of God before it is followed. To put too much stress on the subjective necessity of following one's conscience, without an overwhelming emphasis on the need for conscience certainly to be corrected and directed by Christ, may sanction too much irresponsible individualism in the name of conscience.'

3. There is also the question of the '*mala fide*' conscience. If religious liberty is the social faculty of acting religiously, as many say 'according to conscience', and in fact I am acting against the dictates of my own conscience, could I demand freedom for my acting '*mala fide*'? But, on the other hand, if I lie and say that I am acting according to my conscience, how can society know the real state of my spirit? Must society, in the impossibility of knowing the real facts of my conscience, accord freedom only to the beliefs and deeds which are objectively right? What religious liberty would then be left?

These questions and examples show us clearly that we shall never have a correct and complete notion of religious liberty unless we previously clarify our concepts on 'conscience'.

We think that it is first necessary to establish precisely the meaning of the term itself. What do we mean by the word 'conscience'? Here we have again a question of terminology occasioned by the vagueness and ambiguity of words.

Among the several meanings which the word 'conscience' may have, there are two which concern our particular question. The first is the more precise and technical one, in the sense that conscience is our immanent and native faculty for reaching moral judgments, conclusions and decisions. As truths and principles are known and interpreted by us through our own conscience, it is obvious that, in practice, this faculty becomes for us our last norm and rule of action and decision. We believe that this signification of the word conscience is meant when there is the question of 'primacy' of conscience, for we must primarily follow what our conscience tells us; or, in other words, that the criterion of our own conscience has (for us) primacy over all other criterions. In a transferred sense, but with the same meaning as above, we apply the name of the *faculty* to the *results* of its exercise, and thus we call conscience not only the faculty of reaching conclusions, but also the conclusions themselves, which are frequently named the 'dictates' of conscience. So 'the right to act according to conscience' in short is meant by 'the right to act according to *the dictates* of conscience'.

Another more popular meaning of 'conscience' is that of our internal or spiritual faculties and activities in general. Thus 'conscience' is the whole area of our thoughts, feelings, desires, volitions and decisions, at least as far as they do not take concrete form in external and social deeds. We think that this is the meaning of expressions such as 'the sanctuary of conscience'. By this we do not point out precisely the concrete faculty for reaching decisions or judgments, but generally our whole internal 'world', everything which is and occurs within our spirit or, in very plain language, 'our private and personal business'. Let us now try to apply these notions to the problems of religious liberty.

If we take 'conscience' in the rather popular signification of our internal and spiritual world, it is obvious that, in this sense, 'liberty of conscience' cannot be fully equivalent to religious liberty in general which includes many external, collective and corporate activities. Nevertheless, in this sense, 'liberty of conscience' may be one part of religious liberty, that is, the freedom to determine one's own faith and creed and to think, worship and act according to this faith, inasmuch as these activities do not presuppose the exercise of other specifically different human rights. This is the meaning in which we spoke of 'liberty of conscience' in the previous chapter, employing the word 'conscience' in the general sense of our internal 'selves'.

If we take the word 'conscience' in the more precise sense of our faculty of reaching judgments, conclusions and decisions, could we call social religious freedom 'liberty of conscience'? In spite of the fact that there are some theologians who accept this terminology, our response is negative. The matter is important, for it does not involve a mere question of terms. This is a substantial problem, the problem of knowing whether 'the dictates of our conscience' can constitute an element of our conception of social religious liberty. Social religious freedom is a *social* freedom, i.e. a faculty which we can ask society to respect and which society must be able to respect. How can we then imagine the ability of society to respect our faculty *to follow the dictates of our conscience*? How can societies, states, individuals, corporations, know 'the dictates of our conscience'? Obviously, only through us telling them. And if we lie? This is nonsense. Society cannot possibly allow its respect of religious freedom to depend on facts that it cannot investigate. May I be allowed to note that this is a mistake very similar and parallel to the traditional Roman Catholic sophism of the 'rights of the truth' adduced for violating religious liberty. Civil society is as incompetent to decide what is truth and what is religious error as it is to pronounce which conscience is right and which is wrong. All are matters far away and above the knowledge of society.

The consequence of this is that the problems of the 'mistaken' conscience and of the '*mala fide*' conscience are entirely irrelevant to *social* religious freedom. Of course, these problems may be very important and they are in fact for questions of *inner* freedom, for internal freedom is not licence and God's gift of liberty is not given to us for irresponsible use. These problems are also important for the *moral* responsible exercise *even of our social liberty*. But these moral rules and the consequent investigation of our conscience cannot be subject to the competence of society. Society must have other criteria, different from that of knowing what the dictates of our conscience are, to ascertain when it should or should not respect our freedom.

Social religious liberty is on the level of human justice. Now, human justice is essentially imperfect and limited. It is clearly impossible for human law, in most cases, to reach perfect justice. For instance, the general principle of punishing criminals is to punish them in proportion to their real culpability, but civil society can do this only very roughly, merely according to external evidence. Therefore social institutions are frequently put in a dilemma: they must either fail altogether to reflect justice even in its minimal and supreme principles, or adapt justice to the imperfections of external human relations. Obviously they must take the second alternative and so at least comply with the most essential demands of justice.

Applying this general consideration to our particular case, it is completely impossible for society to penetrate the secret of conscience and to inquire into human hearts. Thus society is forced either to deny or ignore religious liberty or to abstain from investigating the state of consciences. In other words, society must presume that everybody is acting in all good faith concerning his religious beliefs.

Consequently the elements which enter into consideration for determining the practical enactment of the principle of religious liberty within human society are not the *internal* questions of the erring or bad conscience, but, on the one hand, the society's duty to recognize and respect the higher human loyalties and, on the other hand, the necessity of doing this in the frame of social harmony.

The fact that divine revelation is absolute truth gives us the right to compare this truth with someone's convictions and to conclude that the latter are wrong and, consequently, that the conscience which dictated such convictions is an erring one. But that fact does not give us the right to impede that conscience from being wrong. This is the risk of liberty, a risk that even God (who knows the conscience) is willing to take. *A fortiori* should the society (to which consciences are an impenetrable mystery) take this risk.

We very well understand that some theologians are reluctant to abandon traditional reasoning based on the '*bona fide*' conscience, for this argument in defence of the 'erring in all good faith', with all the romantic atmosphere of the last century, was beautiful in 'apologetics', while the principle of respecting *all* consciences, without knowing if they are right or wrong, good or bad, could give the impression that we are defending fools and rascals. The trouble is that the beautiful argument is false, and the less beautiful is the only correct one.

In spite of what we have said, society can and should, nevertheless, do something in affairs of the conscience, namely:

(*a*) Firstly, it is a social duty to educate conscience and its enlightenment so that it becomes easier for it to find the correct answers to conscience problems and more difficult to act against one's own conscience. This, far from being an unjust limitation of freedom, effectively contributes to its better exercise.

(*b*) Society and State may, quite independently of the good or bad consciences of the citizens, impede or limit some activities, even exercised on grounds of religion, which are plainly contrary to the generally accepted moral standards or to the correctly understood common good. Society should of course respect 'the sanctuary of conscience' or, more precisely, it has no means to enter into it; but, on the other hand, it has the right and the duty to protect essential moral and material goods of the community, in spite of the 'dictates' of some consciences. We shall study this problem in our Part III.

4

RELIGIOUS LIBERTY AND HUMAN RIGHTS[1]

MENTION OF religious liberty will immediately call to mind 'human rights'. In this respect some questions have to be answered. Should we say that religious liberty is a human right? Is religious liberty a part of the general concept of freedom and human rights, or is religious liberty unique and distinctive? In what sense may we say that religious liberty is interrelated with all other human rights? The Central Committee of the WCC has said that 'religious freedom is the condition and guardian of all true freedom'. Is this true?

1. *Religious liberty is a fundamental human right*

We said above that social religious freedom is a social *faculty*, which is a larger notion than that of a mere legal right.[2] Nevertheless it would seem that it is *also* a right, and ecumenical statements speak frequently of religious liberty as 'the rights of religious freedom'.

Some theologians, however, do not like the stress put on the legal element of religious liberty and underline the relative importance of 'rights' in Christian revelation. One of them, for instance, says

> 'The New Testament justice, if there be such a thing, to me is the stress of God's complete concern for each and all to have his or their

---

[1] It is well known that the conception and practice of human rights have been subject to many changes and developments in history. A historical survey (otherwise most useful and interesting) falls outside the scope of the present discussion and we limit ourselves here to the consideration of human rights which is current today.

[2] The notion of 'social faculty' also infers that religious freedom should not be protected merely by *legal provisions*. Legal provisions are useful; but they are insufficient and, in some cases, unnecessary.

fullest opportunity in creative service and fulfilment. It is therefore love's concern for orderly opportunity for each and all within the social order. Rights can be conceived of as being bestowed upon people by God's concern for them and as the practical outworking of Christian love in fostering and maintaining satisfactory community relations. The stress on rights itself, however, in the very spirit of the stress, is sub- or anti-Christian.'

We certainly fully agree with the idea that the New Testament is a Covenant of Love and not a Covenant of Rights and that, therefore, the *total stress* of the Christian revelation is from the point of view of Christ's ultimate concern for the people rather than for their rights. Consequently, we also think that the essential notion of the '*libertas christiana*' is not centred on rights, but on love. Nevertheless, we should not forget that the freedom of which we are speaking here, and that which ecumenical bodies demand in their statements, is not the '*libertas christiana*' but the social external faculty which is also a human right. We do not wish *to stress* the importance of rights and to put them, so to say, among the essentials of Christian revelation. Far from it. We only wish to say that there are human rights which are 'God-given rights' and which 'are His will for all men';[1] and that Christianity and Church must have concern for justice and rights for all people, especially those discriminated against. We do not think that this is to put too much stress on 'rights' but simply to follow the Christian calling for the defence of the God-given human dignity in the social context. That is why the Assembly of the WCC at Evanston carefully considered its competence to proclaim that 'a call for the protection *of human rights* is all the more insistent in this age when, in various parts of the world, totalitarianism . . . oppresses the freedom of men and of institutions. . . . A system of justice which defends the rights and dignity of the human person *is fundamental*.'[2]

The formulation, which occurs very frequently, that religious liberty is a human right, is incomplete and in itself meaningless, for *all* rights are human. What is really meant is that religious liberty is a *fundamental* human right, i.e. a right which, having

[1] Cf. Second Assembly of the WCC, Evanston, 1954: p. 140 of Evanston *Report*.
[2] *Ibid.* Report on 'Christians in the Struggle for World Community', p. 130 ff.

its roots in the human race as such, belongs to every human being and should be universally recognized and respected.[1]

This universality and fundamental character of religious freedom has been repeatedly proclaimed by the ecumenical movement, particularly by the Amsterdam Assembly:

'The rights of religious freedom herein declared shall be recognized and observed for all persons without distinction as to race, colour, sex, language or religion, and without imposition of disabilities by virtue of legal provision or administrative acts.'[2]

Similarly the Latin–European Churches:

'The Conference affirms that religious freedom is universal, belonging to every man, to every church, and in every country, without regard to any local circumstances, and that this principle cannot be invalidated, either before the law or in effect, because of the differing conditions in a particular country.'[3]

We do not think it necessary to insist upon this point for it seems there is a general ecumenical conviction that, as said at the Eastern Asia Conference, 'the most fundamental freedom is religious freedom'.[4]

Nevertheless, before we continue our study, we would like to make an important observation on terminology: 'human rights' does not mean *only* individual rights, but social; and particularly the interaction of the two and the creation of either by the other. There is namely the danger that, through a literal translation from the French *'Droits de l'Homme'*, and still more as a relic of the old individualistic liberal tradition of the French Revolution, we consider as a human right exclusively the right of the individual. On the contrary, human rights in general and religious liberty in particular, are social in a double sense: social, because they are

[1] Some theologians do not like *the term* 'human rights', which seems to them to be difficult and to obscure the general concept of rights. There is perhaps a point there. Nevertheless, we wish to note: (1) that the phrase 'human rights' has been universally accepted and received both in the secular and the ecclesiastical terminology; (2) that, as we say in the text, the commonly accepted meaning of 'human rights' seems to be that of those rights which derive from the very 'structure' of man, and which, therefore, should be always protected and safeguarded. This generally accepted notion seems sufficiently clear and need not enter into the theological question of the essential nature and source of such rights.
[2] First Assembly of the WCC, Amsterdam, 1948, Declaration on Religious Liberty, pp. 97–9 of official *Report*.
[3] Conference of the Protestant Churches of the Latin European Countries, Chambon-sur-Lignon, France, 1958, Resolutions on Religious Liberty.
[4] Eastern Asia Conference, Bangkok, 1949.

not only individual, but also collective and corporative; social, because their exercise takes place in the social context and is conditioned by it. Man being essentially a *social* being, the distinction between collective rights and individual rights is, of course, a merely intellectual category, which is necessary in systematic analysis, but which should not be considered as taking place in human life. Since the nature of man is a social nature which requires group life for his individual fulfilment, it would follow that the respect for the individual rights requires also a respect for the group rights.

2. *Religious liberty is a distinctive human right*

This explicit assertion of the New Delhi Assembly that 're-ligious freedom may be considered as a *distinctive* human right'[1] seems to us of particular importance. First of all, it must be made clear that the New Delhi Assembly is dealing with *the Christian view* of a general human right. To be a distinctive or a unique human right means that religious liberty is not merely the application of the common human rights to religious matters or activities, but that it is a human right specifically different from the others, with its own peculiar notions and contents.

It must be said that this 'distinctiveness' of the human right of religious liberty is not accepted by all thinkers, not even by all ecumenical theologians.

First, many 'secularist' or 'humanist' scholars do not recognize the religious 'sphere' as something different or superior to the other human activities. For them there exist merely the general and fundamental human rights of freedom of thought, freedom of expression and communication, of public meetings, of associa-tion, etc. That these fundamental human rights concern religion, or science, or politics, or selling beauty products, is indifferent to them and considered as completely irrelevant to the essence and import of the human rights in themselves.

This position is, we think, entirely wrong; against what has been said, *the substance of religious liberty* plainly justifies its essential specification. We said above that religion means, at least, our essential and eternal relations with our God, Creator,

[1] Third Assembly of the WCC, New Delhi, 1961, Statement on Religious Liberty: pages 159–61 of the *New Delhi Report*.

Redeemer and Sanctifier. This relationship puts man on a transcendental level very much superior to all the other human relationships, be these of political, social, industrial or commercial kind, with which other human rights are concerned. Human activities, which are not religious or, at least, not exclusively religious, are always conditioned by social togetherness and by the necessary limitations of community life. This is not the case concerning 'pure' religious liberty, for our essential relations with the divinity entirely transcend the temporal horizon. We say 'pure' religious liberty, or liberty of conscience, for we recognize that the mixed religious freedoms, i.e. those which presuppose the exercise of other human rights, are also conditioned by social exigences, although the particular transcendency of their religious element should in no way be neglected. This essential transcendency of the human relations with God fully justifies, in our opinion, the consideration of religious liberty as a distinctive and unique human right.

When ecumenical theologians are reluctant to consider religious liberty as an independent and distinctive human right, they do it from a quite different angle. They rather take the line of one of our most learned advisers, who explains his opinion as follows:

'It seems doubtful whether *religious* liberty by itself, apart from freedom of thought, inquiry and expression, and freedom of choice generally, should be singled out for defence. Christian faith is concerned with the whole man. We are not interested in defending the prerogatives of churches. But to limit the discussion to religious liberty appears to lay us open to the charge of special pleading. Application of the principle of non-coercion embraces the whole field. The effect is weakened if one segment only is singled out. In this scientific age it may be important to show that freedom for scientific inquiry and for the exercise of religious faith rest on much the same premises.'

In this opinion we find some insights with which we fully agree. Indeed, Christian faith 'is concerned with *the whole man*' and not exclusively with the religious man. Moreover, Christianity should by no means use religious liberty as an instrument 'of special pleading' for defending 'the prerogatives of the churches'. This is entirely correct and, because of this, the World Council of Churches has always demanded not only religious freedom, but also generally 'a system of justice which defends the rights and dignity of the human person'.[1] Because of this, too, the ecumenical movement, far from defending the prerogatives of the churches, has often stated that 'in pleading for such rights of religious freedom we do not ask for any privilege to be granted to Christians that is denied to others . . . ; the rights which Christian discipleship demands are such as are good for all men.'[2]

Nevertheless, we do think that we ought to 'single out' religious liberty, not only for defence, but primarily on the level of concepts. Is religious liberty simply a particular case of human rights, in so far as these can have 'religion' as their subject? Or, on the contrary, is it, in its own concept, a distinctive human right, specifically different from the others, although interrelated with them and, in some cases, forming with them a particular complex? We think that the second answer is the correct one, for all the other human rights concern essentially pure human relations, or the relationship of man to society, while religious liberty concerns essentially divine-human relations, or the relationship of God to humanity, thus introducing a transcendent element which changes radically the essence of the right in question.[3] If this is so, as we believe, we would say that Christian faith is indeed concerned with the whole man and with all his rights, but proportionately to the different nature of these rights. We do not hold, therefore, that the particular concern for religious freedom, based on its divine value, could constitute a charge of special pleading.

As for reasons in favour of religious liberty, we should investigate (and we will do this in our Part II), whether the arguments employed apply *equally* to religious freedom and to other freedoms, or whether they apply *primarily* to religious liberty in such a special way that religious liberty becomes in a certain measure the foundation of the other liberties. If the second alternative follows, the singling out of religious liberty for defence does not weaken but, on the contrary, strengthens the general argument.

Finally we think that, strategically, experience shows that all liberties (religious included) stand together and fall together; but

[1] Second Assembly of the WCC, Evanston, 1954; Report on 'Christians in the Struggle for World Community'.
[2] The World Conference on Church, Community and State, Oxford, 1937; Report on 'The Universal Church and the World of Nations'. First Assembly of the WCC, Amsterdam, 1948, Declaration on Religious Liberty.
[3] Some point out that this conception of the religious relationship is not that of many non-Christians, which consider it as purely immanent. We completely agree. We are giving here the *Christian* point of view concerning this question.

that the safeguard of the other freedoms mostly depends on the recognition and practice of religious freedom.

3. *Religious liberty is interrelated with all other human rights*

This interrelation between 'freedoms of every kind' and particularly of religious freedom with all other human rights has been proclaimed by the ecumenical bodies.[1]

As we said in a previous chapter,[2] with the sole exception of that kind of religious liberty which consists of the exemption from every social compulsion in our essential and private relations with God, all the other religious freedoms also presuppose the exercise of other human rights, particularly those enumerated in the New Delhi Statement. Consequently, in most of the cases, there is some dynamic interaction between religious liberty and human rights, as we see, for instance, when the freedom of religious expression and communication presupposes both our religious liberty and our fundamental human right of social expression.

But this interrelation takes place not only between religious freedom and each of the single human rights, but also between religious liberty and all the other freedoms generally, or considered as a whole. Someone said that Christian thought has to proclaim the 'rights' of God (of course, in the sense of his absolute sovereignty) as the foundation and perfection of the 'rights of man'. This doubtless means that, consistent with the need of human community, society must respect the prior ends of man and God's Lordship over human kind. This being so, religious liberty and all other human liberties are, in principle and in experience, inevitably interlocked. This is probably what the Latin–European Churches meant by saying that the dignity and rights of man, 'so greatly threatened in the world today, will never be fully safeguarded until the full exercise of religious freedom is respected'.[3] Or with the similar statement of the Eastern Asia Conference that 'nations are not truly free unless they

---

[1] Cf. Third Assembly of the WCC, New Delhi, 1961, Statement on Religious Liberty, No. 10; Second Meeting of the Central Committee of the WCC, Chichester, 1949, Statement on Religious Liberty; Second Assembly of the WCC, Evanston, 1954, Report on 'Christians in the Struggle for World Community'.

[2] Cf. ch. 2, p. 24 ff.

[3] Conference of the Protestant Churches of the Latin European Countries, Chambon-sur-Lignon, France, 1958, Resolutions on Religious Freedom.

recognize that each citizen has the right to decide for himself what religion he will profess'.[1] But this leads us to the last point of this chapter, namely that

4. *Religious liberty is the foundation and guardian of all human rights*

'Religious freedom is the foundation of all freedom.'[2] 'Religious freedom is the condition and guardian of all true freedom.'[3] These and similar expressions are often found in the ecumenical statements. The reason given for these assertions is that 'the fundamental rights of the human person cannot endure except when they are acknowledged as derived from man's relation to God in Christ'.[4] Or, in other terms, that 'only the recognition that man has ends and loyalties beyond the State [we would say, beyond the society in general] will ensure true justice to the human person.'[5]

The habitual shortness of the ecumenical statements obliges us to search in their context for the right explanation of these reasons. First we think it necessary to exclude some exaggerated or mistaken interpretations:

(a) We do not believe that the reasons adduced mean that, *in fact*, there cannot exist fundamental liberties unless religious liberty is recognized. Absolutely speaking, we could imagine some country where, owing to particular circumstances (for instance as a consequence of the existence of an established and majority church), religious liberty of the 'dissidents' is not recognized and, nevertheless, the general regime is rather democratic and respectful of the other civic liberties. This is possible, and perhaps has happened, for instance, in some epochs of the British history.

(b) Neither do we think that, on the level of principles, it would be impossible for people to defend and establish human rights on other grounds and bases than the religious basis or religious freedom. It would seem that some philosophical or historical considerations could lead to the necessity of fundamental liberties as a condition of the health of the human community.

What we consider as the correct interpretation of the above in-

---

[1] Eastern Asia Conference, Bangkok, 1949.
[2] Conference of the Latin European Churches, Chambon-sur-Lignon, *ibid.*
[3] Central Committee of the WCC, Chichester, 1949, Statement on Religious Liberty, p. 15 of *Minutes and Reports*.
[4] Eastern Asia Conference, Bangkok, 1949.
[5] Central Committee of the WCC, Chichester, 1949, *ibid.*, p. 15 of *Minutes and Reports*.

dicated ecumenical affirmations is, that, as a matter of fact, the respect for the highest values of loyalties of man (which are the religious ones) will be the final 'test' and also the best guarantee of the respect for all other human values. If, for instance, a totalitarian state does not recognize even the most sacred sphere of religion and the most intimate human autonomy, it will most probably not stop before other less important values and less intimate spheres. In this sense it seems perfectly correct to affirm that, if society does not respect religion and its liberty, one does not have any security that the rest will be respected.

5

OTHER RELIGIOUS, PHILOSOPHICAL AND POLITICAL CONCEPTIONS OF RELIGIOUS LIBERTY

WE SAID above[1] that, although the social religious freedom demanded by ecumenical bodies is not any kind of specific Christian freedom, nevertheless *our concept* of it is definitely Christian inasmuch as its extension and contents correspond to our Christian insights.

Many non-Christian minds have other conceptions of religious liberty, resulting from their different religious, philosophical or political insights. For them, religious freedom separates in many cases very much from the Christian conception. Moreover, we must recognize that, even for us, 'Christian liberty' is something different from religious freedom, as it has been explained in chapter I of this Part. Besides, we Christians do not regard the Christian belief, in individual or corporate expression, as merely a religion parallel to other religions. Consequently, an understanding of *religious* liberty requires analysis from a Hindu or Moslem angle as well. We think, therefore, that the study of the main non-Christian notions of religious freedom will help us to a better understanding of our own Christian conception of the same.

I. *Non-Christian religious conceptions of religious freedom*

Not a few ecumenical theologians insist with good reason on the need for considering the question of religious liberty as understood by other non-Christian religions, especially in connection with their renewal in the newly independent Asian and African countries. Various outstanding contributions to this study have been

[1] Cf. above, ch. I, pp. 18–19.

made by distinguished specialists,[1] and we refer to them for a deeper knowledge of this problem. In this short study we must limit ourselves to a few key considerations.

Of course, the idea of religious liberty is in no way the same in the greatest non-Christian religions of Islam, Hinduism and Buddhism. In spite of these differences there is an element which appears as common to those three great religions. We would say that this element, in contrast to the Christian religion, is constituted by a difference of stress or emphasis. The Christian religion, owing doubtless to our Lord's commandment to evangelize the whole world, very much emphasizes the freedom of witness, preaching and teaching among all men, even among those who are not *born* in a Christian environment and who do not belong, so to speak, to 'the Christian society'. This was not the emphasis of the great non-Christian religions. They put stress on the freedom to *conserve* the faith in which one has been born. To take the example of Hinduism, the very word *jati* (birth), which is used in all Indian languages for caste, indicates that Hindus came to accept that there was something determinative about birth, in that one was born in a family that settled for him the social and religious status that was to be his.[2]

This explains also the paramount importance of the social and family status in the great non-Christian religions. In Islam, for instance, religion embraces the totality of social life. The community (*ummah*) and loyalty of the individual to this community (which is both political and religious) become matters of vital religious concern. In the traditional orthodox Muslim thinking, separation of religious faith from affairs of society was unthinkable. Therefore, changing faith, for a Muslim, is, in principle, not only an 'apostasy', but a political '*trahison*' and, similarly, religious propaganda of another faith in a Muslim community meant also a political 'aggression'. Only recently some Muslim teachers began to distinguish between changing faith as 'a matter of mere individual conviction' or as 'an act of revolt against Islam'. In this case, the modern hostile reaction against missionaries of other religions

[1] Cf., for instance: Elmer H. Douglas, 'The Theological Position of Islam concerning Religious Liberty', *The Ecumenical Review*, vol. XIII, No. 4, July 1961, pp. 450–62; P. D. Devanandan, 'The Hindu Conception of Religious Liberty in the Melting Pot', *The Ecumenical Review, ibid.*, pp. 439–49.

[2] Cf. Devanandan, 'The Hindu Conception of Religious Liberty in the Melting Pot', *The Ecumenical Review*, vol. XIII, No. 4, July 1961, p. 442.

rather takes the form of defence of religious unity, in a way similar
to that of some Roman Catholic countries.[1] In Hinduism, the importance of the social element in religion is above all reflected in the
identification of 'caste' and religious belonging, so much so that
the word *jati* (birth=caste) also came to be used synonymously with
religion. To be outcasted was to cease to be a Hindu, and con-
trarywise to cease to be a Hindu by becoming an adherent of any
other religion was to incur the penalty of being ostracized by one's
caste-folk. To 'change' one's religion (conversion, to use a Christian term) is to the Hindu, as impossible as to change one's caste.
Consequently, from the Hindu point of view, freedom of religious
opinion does not mean freedom to change one's religion (*svadhar-
ma*, which again is used synonymously for one's caste and one's
religion).[2]

For these non-Christian religions 'freedom of religious opinion'
(which is recognized) is an internal and private affair that does not
affect the social belonging to a religious community or to a religion.
This distinction is the more easy that, for the Asian religions particularly, there is, *within* the religion itself, Hinduism or Buddhism,
a great margin of liberty of opinion in virtue of some mixture of
syncretism and religious relativism, in the sense that every religion
may claim to have a certain amount of truth and no religion can
claim to be in possession of the total religious truth. Thus the
Hindus, for instance, are very proud of their religious 'tolerance',
based upon their concept of *sama darshana* (i.e. religions of equal
value, though different from one another). But this 'tolerance'
based on syncretism and relativism obviates, in their opinion, the
need for 'conversion', for why should religious men quarrel over
the claims of their different creeds? What, after all, does one gain
by changing from one religion to another? This position explains
how this kind of 'tolerance' becomes intolerance and encourages
opposition to all 'conversions' from Hinduism to other religions.[3]

The consequence of this difference in the concept of religious
liberty is somewhat paradoxical. Non-Christians consider Christians as intolerant because they are not able to accept syncretism
and relativism and doubt about their religious truth but, on the
other hand, Christians consider non-Christians as intolerant, for

[1] Cf. Douglas, 'The Theological Position of Islam concerning Religious
Liberty', *ibid.*, pp. 453–4.
[2] Cf. Devanandan, p. 442.   [3] Cf. Devanandan, p. 446.

the latter cannot conceive any reasons for changing beliefs and, as a matter of fact, oppose the liberty of leaving what is considered a national religion for a 'foreign' one. Of course, this way of religious thinking seems to be encouraged in some countries by the feeling and theories of modern Nationalism.

Besides, we must remark that these religions generally make the mistake of confusing 'tolerance' with 'religious liberty'. Although intimately related, both concepts are different, and even the Christian notion of tolerance cannot be identified, either in principle or in practice, with the concrete social and civil faculty of religious liberty.

Considering these restricting elements of the conception of religious liberty as held by the great non-Christian religions, we must say that there is all the more merit in those political leaders (as, for instance, in India and Pakistan) who, in spite of their religious affiliation, and for reasons of their own, defend the same religious freedoms which have been recognized by the Universal Declaration of Human Rights and claimed by Christians.

2. *The Humanistic approach to the conception of religious liberty*

When we speak of a 'humanistic' or secular approach to religious freedom we do not mean that all who represent this tendency are 'atheist' or even vaguely 'deist'. In fact, there are many thinkers who, in spite of their dedicated affiliation to concrete religious confessions, nevertheless consider that on the level of social and political investigations they should put away their personal religious convictions and use methods and concepts common to all thinkers, whatever be their philosophical or religious background. What are then the main lines of this 'humanistic' or 'secular' approach to religious liberty?

We think that the main concern and the point of departure of such authors is what many of them call 'a common civil life'. For them, common civil life means the necessity for men to live and dwell 'with' others, i.e. peaceful togetherness in society. If this peaceful togetherness is to be secured, there must first of all be 'rules of social fair play' accepted generally by society and enforced by the State. The most important of these rules is that every citizen, as well as the associations and corporations created by them, enjoy the freedom of developing their activities of any kind, with full respect for the liberties of others and in the general harmony of the social context. These authors generally think that the fundamental task and mission of the civil society consists of guaranteeing this social harmony of the free exercise of activities of all.

Among these activities of any kind there are too, of course, the religious activities. In this particular point history has shown us that, in all epochs, people understood differently what should be their religious beliefs and attitudes. This originated in what has been called 'religious pluralism', which has become of particular importance in the modern world.

If we now apply the general principle of the peaceful social harmony to the fact of religious pluralism, the consequence will be the particular need of guaranteeing freedom for all in religious matters. Owing to powerful and strong emotions which religion often occasioned, and to the sad experience of so many bloody fights and wars, this religious social harmony can only be secured when civil society guarantees to every religious confession the freedom of developing normally and at the same time prevents a particular religion hindering the freedom of the others.

This social religious harmony can only be realized by a wholly impartial 'arbiter'. This being obviously the civil society, in particular the State, secular thinkers deduce that the State, to be perfectly impartial in religious matters, must be completely alien to every religious conviction. We say alien to every religious conviction and not only to a particular confession because, for these humanists, the civil religious harmony also demands the freedom of the non-believers as well as the freedom of the members of different confessions. Therefore—they say—the impartial arbiter of this religious harmony must be indifferent to every religious consideration. The political consequence of this position is that the State must be entirely separated from churches or similar religious bodies in the sense that the various public activities of civil society ought to be devoid of any religious signification.

It is not our task to judge this 'secular' notion of religious liberty, but to compare it with the ecumenical conception. This comparison shows some analogies and some, still greater, differences.

First of all, Christian thought fully accepts this concern for social peace and the principle that the harmony of the liberties of all is one of the main tasks of the civil society. Furthermore, the general idea of the necessity of an 'arbitration' by the civil society for guaranteeing the legitimate interests and rights of the various groups is also agreed on by the Christian spirit. Finally, the ecumenical conviction is also, as we shall see later, that freedom of religion includes freedom to have no religion and that, therefore, the concept of religious liberty must be such as to be compatible with this right.

Nevertheless, the differences between the Christian and the 'secular' concept of religious liberty are still greater than their analogies. For us Christians, the essential element which constitutes the notion of freedom is not 'human *togetherness*', but human *dignity*. If wild animals would be able to arrive at some agreement concerning their respective 'liberties', these freedoms would not, nevertheless, have the essential characteristics of the human freedoms, for they would be lacking the element of human dignity, i.e. those superior destinies and loyalties which 'social agreement' may not deny or concede, but only recognize and protect. Of course, this human dignity of which we speak, based on man's eternal destiny and on his essential relationship to God, is *not* the same thing as is meant by the ordinary phrase 'the dignity of man'.

For the same reason, Christian thought does not see in 'religious pluralism' the origin of the idea of religious liberty. Pluralism may be the occasion by which the necessity of religious freedom has appeared with clearer evidence. But religious liberty, in the true and Christian sense of the essential autonomy of the relations between man and God, does not depend exclusively on the fact of pluralism.

As for the State's competence concerning religious liberty as it is considered by the secular position, it seems to us at the same time too limited and too large. Too limited, for we do not think that the State can be fully indifferent to religion. Too large, for this competence of arbitration rests on the power of declaring and granting the rights of each citizen, while the Christian thought denies the State's faculty of *granting* fundamental human rights, which, on the contrary, should always be *recognized* by the civil society. But this consideration leads us to the next section.

3. *The understanding of religious freedom by political systems*

Owing to the impossibility of studying all the modern political systems we must limit ourselves to the investigation of their *main types*.

The first one is the *totalitarian* type. Ecumenical bodies gave a rather complete description of totalitarianism: 'It teaches that in order to gain a social or political end everything is permitted; it maintains the complete self-sufficiency of man; it sets political power in the place of God; it denies the existence of absolute moral standards superior to the authority of the State; it moulds the minds of the young in a pattern opposed to the message of the Gospel; it sanctions the use of all manner of means to overthrow all other views and ways of life.'[1]

The totalitarian State, then, claims for itself *all* authority and considers itself as the only source of morality and justice. In the sphere of 'beings', it denies that there is One God, who is not only independent from, but Lord of the State; and that there is the other, man, who has higher loyalties than those due to the civil society. In the sphere of principle, it denies that there are eternal principles which even the State must obey. In a word, the State is the Authority, every authority, and the Law, every law.

The consequence of this for the conception of religious liberty is evident. There is no God Lord of the State, there is no man with eternal loyalties. Therefore all human activities, including the religious ones, are completely submitted to the State's authority.

This general principle is perfectly compatible in practice with many forms, all of them similar in appearance to some kind of religious liberty. The totalitarian State, if it considers it useful, may supremely decide to accord some of the religious freedoms and even promulgate constitutional provisions thereon. It can even 'protect' the churches and take the form of a 'Gallican' or 'Josephinist' State, and intervene in the life of the religious bodies 'under the guise of religion'.[2]

All these forms are accidental for totalitarianism. The only essential principle is that the State is the only origin of justice and the unique authority which can grant or deny rights and freedoms, consequently also religious freedoms. The State may then, without any other norm or principle than its own utility, grant or limit or deny altogether religious liberty.

The ecumenical attitude in face of totalitarianism is well known.

---

[1] Central Committee of the WCC, Chichester, 1949: *Minutes and Reports*, p. 15.

[2] Second Assembly of the WCC, Evanston, 1954, Report on 'Christians in the Struggle for World Community': *Report*, p. 130 ff.

'The totalitarian doctrine is a false doctrine.'[1] 'Any political system which degrades human personality, makes use of it in any way as a mere instrument, or hinders its free expression, is anti-Christian and anti-human.'[2] 'A State which destroys human personality or human associations, or subordinates them to its own ends, is . . . incompatible with the Christian understanding of life.'[3]

Concerning the particular case of religious freedom, it is obvious that the main Christian objection to the totalitarian position is not that various religious freedoms may be violated under such a political system, but the fundamental totalitarian principle that there is no law, no loyalty and no dignity superior to the State. This is the fundamental opposition between Christianity and Totalitarianism: that this denies 'those God-given rights which are his will for all men'.[4] As the First Assembly of the World Council of Churches stated, 'it is presumptuous for the State to assume that it can grant or deny fundamental rights. It is for the State to embody these rights in its own legal system and to ensure their observance in practice.'[5]

In opposition to the totalitarian States we could speak of those which are generally called 'liberal' or 'democratic'. But this terminology conceals deep practical differences of attitude concerning religious liberty and therefore we must distinguish between States which are 'indifferent' to religion, those who explicitly or implicitly accept religious insights and those who profess a concrete religious confession.

The 'indifferent' State is frequently called a 'secular' State. Here again we encounter difficulty in the use of the terms. Many speak of the 'secular' State, but, in employing the same term, they often mean very different things.

First of all there is the secular State of the old French style, which claims to be 'indifferent' to religion, but in fact is hostile to

[1] Central Committee of the WCC, Chichester, 1949: *Minutes and Reports*, p. 15.
[2] First Evangelical Conference of Latin-America, Buenos Aires, 1949.
[3] The World Conference on Church, Community and State, Oxford, 1937, Additional Report of the Section on Church and State.
[4] Second Assembly of the WCC, Evanston, 1954, Report on 'Christians in the Struggle for World Community': *ibid*.
[5] The First Assembly of the WCC, Amsterdam, 1948, Report on 'The Church and the International Disorder': *Report*, p. 93.

it. Proclaiming that religion is, as they used to say, 'a private business', such a State systematically eliminates religion from social life, thus ignoring the necessary social dimension of religious freedom. Such kind of 'secular' or '*laic*' State is generally rejected by all ecumenical thinkers.

Quite different is that other kind of 'secular' State which may be indifferent to religion, but never hostile to it. In this case, 'indifference' means, rather than something negative, a positive and careful respect for all the possible attitudes of citizens concerning religion, from allegiance to a very determinate religious confession or church to atheistic rejection of every religious belief. Such a secular State intends to guarantee full freedom for everybody in matters of religion. Some authors think that this kind of State should not be called '*laic*' or secular, but should be included in another category, where religion is neither prohibited nor eliminated, nor officially promulgated, but is *voluntary*, a matter of free choice by each person. Although not all Christians consider this kind of State as the best possible, it seems that it is generally accepted as being completely correct and compatible with the Christian principles on religious liberty.

Following the terminology of Dr John A. Mackay[1] in his study of the basic attitudes nations can take toward religion, we see that, besides the 'demoniac' (totalitarian) nations, and the 'secular' nations, there are the 'covenant nations' which grow out of an original loyalty and devotion to God and continue to draw upon their origins for strength. The notion of religious liberty which these 'covenant' nations have will obviously depend on their religious allegiance, even if it is not that of a particular concrete confession; and it must be recognized that this confessional allegiance may, in some cases, imply dangers to religious freedom. Nevertheless we may say that, in line with general principles, this conception of religious liberty will be most similar to that of Christian thought. In effect, the recognition of God's Lordship and of human loyalties superior to the social relations will help those States more easily to respect and guarantee all legitimate kinds of religious freedom. Furthermore, if such a State, without any discrimination even towards those who have no faith, contributes

[1] Dr John A. Mackay, former President of the Theological Seminary, Princeton, USA.

to the social improvement of religious insights and convictions, this attitude, far from being contrary to religious liberty, will help to develop this maturity of judgment and customs and of a responsible sense of social life which constitutes the internal presupposition of every external freedom.

Finally, there are those States which accept some concrete confession and in which the Church or another similar body of a non-Christian religion is in some way connected with the State. It must be said that on this kind of State the opinion of Christians is clearly divided, for there are many who resolutely stand for the principle of 'a free Church in a free State',[1] while many others think that 'the freedom essential for the Church can in fact exist both in Churches organized as free associations under the general laws of a country or as established Churches in an organic or otherwise special connection with the State.'[2]

It seems obvious, particularly concerning our problem, that countries which officially profess a particular religion *may have* a correct conception of religious liberty. We think, for instance, that the British understanding of religious freedom in the modern times is a perfect one, in spite of having an established Church.

Once this possibility is gladly recognized, we must, nevertheless, point out some dangers of this situation for the right understanding of religious liberty.

The first and most frequent danger is that of confusing the common civil good with the religious welfare in the sense understood by the official religion. If, for instance, religious unity and national prosperity are considered as essentially interlocked, the State will be inclined to defend religious unity and to prohibit 'dissidence'. Think, for instance, of Spain and Burma.

The second danger concerns, paradoxically, the very 'protected' or established Church. The First Assembly of the WCC solemnly proclaimed that 'every religious organization . . . has the right to determine its policies and practices for the accomplishment of its chosen purposes'.[3] Unfortunately this is not always the case with the 'established churches'.

[1] Cf., for instance, the *Statement of the Federal Council of the Churches of Christ (U.S.A.)*, Pittsburg, 1944.
[2] The World Conference on Church, Community and State, Oxford, 1937, Additional Report of the Section on Church and State.
[3] The First Assembly of the WCC, Amsterdam, 1948, Declaration on Religious Liberty.

A final danger relates in particular to the non-Christian religions. In the case of some of these great non-Christian religions, as for instance Islam or Buddhism, which become the religion of the State, it is obvious that the State concerned would participate in the restricted notion of religious liberty of those religions and, therefore, regard with suspicion and hostility the freedom of 'propaganda' of so-called 'foreign' religions, and still more the right or freedom of conversion or of abandoning the religion of one's own birth. Frequently, legal and administrative limitations of religious liberty must recognize this religious origin.

II

WHY CHRISTIANS DEMAND
RELIGIOUS LIBERTY

I

ARE THERE THEOLOGICAL GROUNDS FOR RELIGIOUS LIBERTY?

THE TITLE of this Second Part seems to imply that Christians as such have specific religious, biblical and theological grounds for demanding that religious liberty be recognized and respected by the civil society. In fact, the existence of such particular Christian reasons in favour of religious freedom has been repeatedly proclaimed by ecumenical bodies.[1] Nevertheless and although there is ecumenical conviction that 'we hold a distinctive Christian basis for religious liberty',[2] on the other side it is generally admitted in ecumenical circles that 'there has not yet emerged a consensus concerning the theological and ethical reasons why religious freedom must be defended.'[3]

For our part, we must confess that the investigation of the Christian grounds for religious liberty has constituted the main subject of the studies and discussions of the Commission on Religious Liberty; and that there have been registered the most numerous and most important differences of opinion, which is not surprising, considering the differences of theological traditions among the member churches. We do not intend to solve all difficulties here and to formulate the theological foundation of religious liberty in such a manner that could receive a unanimous ecumenical 'consensus'. Our task, by far the more modest, is that of presenting to the churches the results of our discussions,

[1] Cf. for instance: First Assembly of the WCC, Amsterdam, 1948, Declaration on Religious Liberty; The World Conference on Church, Community and State, Oxford, 1937, Report on 'The Universal Church and the World of Nations'; Declaration of the First Evangelical Conference of Latin America, Buenos Aires, 1949; Third Assembly of the WCC, New Delhi, 1961, Statement on Religious Liberty, etc., etc.

[2] Third Assembly of the WCC, New Delhi, 1961, Statement on Religious Liberty, No. 3.

[3] Central Committee of the WCC, Nyborg, 1958, Approved Programme of Study on Religious Liberty: *Minutes and Reports*, p. 84.

underlining the main points of theological tension as well as the significant agreements reached; and to propose the questions which could be the matter of fruitful study and discussion by the churches.

To begin with, there is a conviction on which we find complete ecumenical agreement, namely that social religious liberty, such as the ecumenical movement demands, *is not a revealed truth*. This ecumenical agreement is indirectly confirmed by several official statements when they say that religious liberty is 'an *implication* of the faith of the Church';[1] 'an *implication* of the Christian faith'.[2] Consequently, not an *explicitly* revealed truth. But if such statements indirectly recognize that social religious liberty is not an explicitly revealed truth, they at the same time proclaim that liberty of religion 'has its deepest foundations in the Gospel of Jesus Christ';[3] i.e. that our Christian faith *implies* the exigency of social religious freedom; in other words, that there is some 'nexus' between Christian revelation and religious liberty. Our prime question is, therefore, to investigate this 'nexus' or to see exactly how religious liberty is implied in the Christian revelation.

Particularly concerning the study of the *biblical texts*, we may also register another ecumenical agreement. Scholars generally recognize, with Amos Wilder, that the Scriptures provide 'unshakable grounding' for religious liberty.[4] As for the *method* of investigating the Bible, there is also unanimous consensus of opinion that the study cannot be confined to those single scriptural passages which are considered as dealing specifically with Christian freedom, but that it must include—as said the Commission on Religious Liberty—'the full meaning and nature of the Gospel'.[5] Or, as Professor Søe would say, 'it is not single passages in the Bible, it is Christ's whole way of approaching mankind that gives us our lead.'[6] Of course, this general ecumenical opinion should be understood in the sense that, while religious liberty is not to be

---

[1] The World Conference on Church, Community and State, Oxford, 1937, Report on 'The Universal Church and the World of Nations'.

[2] First Assembly of the WCC, Amsterdam, 1948, Declaration on Religious Liberty.

[3] Declaration of the First Evangelical Conference of Latin America, Buenos Aires, 1949.

[4] Amos N. Wilder, '*Eleutheria* in the New Testament and Religious Liberty', *The Ecumenical Review*, vol. XIII, No. 4, July 1961, p. 411.

[5] Commission on Religious Liberty, Spittal Meeting, 1959.

[6] Prof. Søe at the Spittal Meeting. Prof. Søe was a member of the late Commission on Religious Liberty and one of our best advisers.

logically deduced from single biblical texts through some literal hermeneutic, on the other hand it would be going too far to avoid biblical citations which can certainly show the spirit and ethos of the whole revelation. On the contrary, this method of appositely using biblical citations has been employed by the most outstanding specialists.[1]

Concerning logical reasoning in this matter, many advisers were of the opinion that not only in biblical study, but generally in our theological thinking, we should guard against the temptation to resort to abstract deduction, which would be hardly adequate to solve such a complex problem.[2]

Here we come to the great question of ascertaining *in what manner* Scriptures and Theology give us a lead for the foundation of social religious liberty. We must confess that, in this respect, there is no more ecumenical agreement, and that we must register different and, in some cases, opposite traditions. The most discussed point in this context has been that of the *interrelations* between the *inner* Christian freedom with which Christ has set us free and the *social* or external religious freedom which ecumenical bodies claim. The point of departure of our study in this matter was the well-known statement by the Amsterdam Assembly which we must reproduce here:

'While the liberty with which Christ has set men free can neither be given nor destroyed by any government, Christians, because of that inner freedom, are both jealous for its outward expression and solicitous that all men should have freedom in religious life.'[3]

We hope to be true to this text if we present its statements in the following fashion:

(a) Christian liberty, or the liberty with which Christ has set us free, is an *inner* freedom.

(b) Being inner, Christian liberty cannot be given or destroyed by any human power.

(c) Social or external religious liberty is the outward expression of the inner Christian liberty. Social religious liberty can be given (we would say: recognized) or destroyed by human powers. Social religious liberty is not identical with inner Christian freedom.

[1] See, for instance, the above-cited article by Amos N. Wilder; the lecture by Prof. Søe at the Nyborg Meeting of the Central Committee of the WCC, 1958: *The Ecumenical Review*, vol. XI, No. 1, October 1958, pp. 36–42.
[2] Cf. for instance the advice given by the Italian Commission on Religious Liberty.
[3] First Assembly of the WCC, Amsterdam, 1948, Declaration on Religious Liberty, Introduction.

(*d*) Christians demand social religious liberty ('outward expression')
because of the inner Christian liberty.

How far do theologians who participate in the ecumenical
debate agree on these statements?

Firstly, they all agree on the *clear distinction* between Christian
liberty and social religious liberty. We have already spoken of the
ecumenical agreement on this distinction.[1] As one of our advisers
said, one thing is 'what man is able to be in himself, in terms of
spiritual allegiance, convictions as to right and wrong, moral
judgments, personal commitment and desire and purpose on the
one hand', and another quite different thing is 'that which he has
freedom and power to express, to manifest, and to carry into
effect in the social fabric of which he is part'.

Secondly, we also register ecumenical agreement on the affirmation that social religious freedom is the 'outward expression' of the
inner Christian liberty.

On the other hand, a most controversial question is that of
knowing whether Christians should demand this 'outward
expression', or social religious liberty, *because* of the inner
Christian liberty; and, still more, what is the exact meaning of this
'because'.

For some theologians (who seem to be in the minority) this
'because' is altogether a mistake. They think that social religious
liberty (which they sometimes call, in our opinion incorrectly,
'liberty of religious exercise in a State') cannot be claimed on
grounds of the inner Christian freedom. Their main argument is
that both these liberties are *completely* different, so that the one
cannot be the reason for the other.

The great majority of theologians believe, with the Amsterdam
Assembly, that we should demand social religious liberty 'because'
of the inner freedom. Still more, they think that this 'because'
includes several interrelations which complete each other.

The first interrelation proposed is a factual or historical one,
based on the fact that inner freedom can and often is destroyed by
external coercion. As one of these theologians wrote, 'these two
realms interact on each other so that the absolute freedom of
spirit which is postulated is actually maimed and thwarted to some
degree by the psychological constraints which society is able to

[1] Cf. Part I, ch. i, p. 17.

exercise.' The consequence, and not a mere abstract one but of the kind based on the concrete needs of humanity, is that the external coercion which often deprives man of the possibility of acting responsibly in religious matters (inner freedom) is 'a denial of God's intention for man';[1] and consequently, that liberation of external coercion is demanded by the very inner Christian freedom.

There are some who simply deny the force of this argument. Based on the ecumenical statement that 'the liberty with which Christ has set us free can neither be given nor destroyed by any government', they think that inner religious freedom is entirely independent of external freedom. Furthermore, persecutions are announced in the Bible as almost the *normal* situation for the Church in many ways, and the same persecutions purify and strengthen Christianity. Therefore, they conclude, it is wrong to say that inner Christian freedom necessitates social freedom.

Other theologians think that a fundamental distinction is necessary to clarify this point. Concerning an *absolute* need, it seems obvious that inner religious freedom does not, in any way, need the protection of social liberty, for there is no human power able to destroy the very roots of our liberty in Christ. Concerning a *relative* (or '*de facto*') need, they firmly believe that external coercion may actually contradict God's intention in giving man inner freedom. Besides, these theologians think that the inner human power of resisting '*de facto*' external coercion, as well as the beneficial effects of persecution, are often exaggerated. The Reformation spread rapidly and took deep roots in Spain in the sixteenth century, but Philip II and the Spanish Inquisition, *with their external power*, not only succeeded in making martyrs, but also in completely eradicating for centuries the evangelical faith. Henry VIII of England successfully turned a Roman Catholic population into an Anglican one in just a few years, and certainly not merely by external and constrained allegiance. The flourishing and very numerous Christianity of Japan in the seventeenth century was drowned in blood by the Emperors, and the Japanese people forgot for centuries their Christian convictions. Similar examples could be multiplied. They clearly

---

[1] First Assembly of the WCC, Amsterdam, 1948, Report on 'The Church and the Disorder of Society'. Cf. also in the same Assembly the Report on 'The Church and the International Disorder': '. . . what are the essential human rights *if men are to be free to do the Will of God.*'

show that external coercion can quite well have destructive effects on the inner freedom and that persecution, when it is radical, has no such inner purifying and strengthening effects. God may permit in His providence such coercion but His primary intention is that man remains free and, respecting Himself this inner freedom, His will is *a fortiori* that men do the same.

But these considerations lead us to investigate whether there are, between inner Christian freedom and social religious liberty, *essential* interrelations other than the purely factual ones based on the practical need of some external protection for inner liberty.

Does inner freedom *demand in itself* social religious freedom, independently of the fact that external coercion may or may not influence internal freedom?

Many theologians answer affirmatively, based mainly on their conviction, above indicated,[1] that inner and social freedom is not so completely different and independent as some think, particularly because the biblical conception of Christian freedom is not so *exclusively* private and inner.

We very much regret that we are not able to give here a larger exposition of Dr Wilder's article on the matter.[2] We shall indicate, nevertheless, its essentials. For Wilder, 'as the Bible sees man, the freedom in question (Christian liberty) cannot be viewed only as a private and inner freedom'.[3] The inner freedom of the New Testament includes also, in his opinion, the demand that 'human authorities should not trespass upon this final zone of liberty of the creature in what concerns his destiny and his dealings with eternity'.[4]

The reason for this, in Wilder's opinion, is that, for the New Testament, 'the existence of the self[5] is a social-historical existence, and its will and action involves other creatures in a public way. The self is not an atom, its life is not purely 'spiritual', and its relation to God is not only vertical. The primordial freedom of the creature must be allowed a public-historical expression subject to the limits of the divine sovereignty which, indeed, operates in

---

[1] Cf. Part I, ch. 1, p. 17–18 f.

[2] Amos N. Wilder, '*Eleutheria* in the New Testament and Religious Liberty', *The Ecumenical Review*, vol. XIII, No. 4, July 1961, pp. 409–20.

[3] *Ibid.*, p. 413.   [4] *Ibid.*, p. 412.

[5] Wilder notes that he prefers the term 'self' to the term 'soul' because of the latter's wrong identification with individualistic conceptions of man not in keeping with the biblical personal-corporate anthropology. Cf. art. cit., p. 412.

part through the social orders. But the social orders and the civil powers must act here within the terms of their mandate and subject to divine judgment.'[1]

Even Paul's distinctive understanding of Christian freedom has, for Wilder, a clear social-political implication. Here our author recognizes that the 'common view' (at least the German one) is that Paul's understanding of Christian freedom has nothing to do with freedom in its political aspect nor with our modern idea of the inborn freedom of man.[2] He also recognizes that, for superficial observers, Paul's freedom, 'as an aspect of justification, "freedom from the law, sin and death", appears to mean an inner personal freedom of a kind which comes to clearest expression precisely under constraints, denials and persecution'.[3] Nevertheless, Wilder thinks that 'Paul's *eleutheria* is an eschatological freedom operating in the world, in history.'[4] 'In Stoicism and Gnosticism (and in some forms of modern idealism) it is possible to hold a conception of religious freedom and of man in which the soul is indifferent to the structures of the world or to that which is beyond its disposal. But such individualism and a-historicism is not envisaged in the New Testament. Thus Paul's radical view of Christian freedom (cf. also John 8.32 ff. and Jesus' words in Matt. 17.24 as to the freedom of sons)—identified with the life of the Spirit, with *parrhesia*, joy, peace and glory—carries with it an irresistible pressure, and one that is not only "spiritual", upon all orders of the "flesh", whether in Church or in State. That this pressure is defined in terms of love and suffering ("a bruised reed he will not break": cf. the "marks of an apostle" of Paul, II Cor. 12.10–12) does not mean that public and worldly historical interests and patterns are not rudely unsettled and overturned (cf. Acts 19, the impact of the Gospel on Ephesus).'[5]

The conclusions reached by Wilder through this examination of Paul's understanding of Christian liberty are:

(1) In this freedom the ultimate responsibility for choice and decision on the part of the believer is presupposed.

(2) This freedom is not solely inner and private freedom but is understood by Paul as having a *historical-social* and indeed cosmic outreach and effect.

[1] Art. cit., p. 413.
[2] Cf., for instance, Ulrich Neuenschwander, 'Das Verständnis der christlichen Freiheit bei Paulus', *Schweizerische Theologische Umschau* 24 (1954), pp. 104–12. Cited by Wilder, *ibid.*, p. 416.
[3] Art. cit., p. 414.   [4] *Ibid.*, p. 415.   [5] *Ibid.*, pp. 415–16.

(3) The Christian is obliged to recognize the freedom of his fellow-believers in this sense.

(4) *The temporal power* even of the pagan State *is viewed as similarly obliged.*[1]

We may say that this position is accepted by many, if not by all, ecumenical theologians in the sense that they think there is some essential relationship between inner and social freedom, so that the former constitutes a necessity of the latter; and that the inner freedom of the Christian presupposes, if not through mere *conceptual* logicality, at least in virtue of some logicality of Christian attitude, the social respect for the inner maturity it has achieved in man as well as for the community conditions that make it possible for all.[2] However, we should not forget that there are very distinguished ecumenical theologians opposed to Wilder's thesis. We shall study this other opinion in ch. 4 of this Part, pp. 83–90.

The different and even opposite positions of the ecumenical theologians concerning the interrelations between inner Christian freedom and social religious liberty have made it necessary that their theological foundations of religious freedom follow different ways.

Those theologians who recognize essential interrelations between both freedoms believe that the fundamental principle which gives a Christian basis to the social religious liberty is God's will, revealed in the Bible, that man should be free in religious matters, both internally and socially. This insight which, rather than being an *argument* in a dialectic sense, constitutes the whole spirit and heart of the biblical revelation, has two aspects. The first is that the *status* of man, as he has been created, redeemed and called by God, including his personal destiny and his social vocation, relates primarily to the realm of freedom, so that humanity, as it is presented in the biblical revelation, is intelligible only in the hypothesis that the purpose of God is better served by leaving man free to make choices for which he has to bear the

---

[1] Art. cit., p. 416.

[2] Some theologians doubt whether the ordinary 'vocabulary' used here generally by the authors is the most appropriate one. They consider that the word 'inner' is not a very descriptive phrase for the relationships between man and his God vertically conceived. Moreover, the phrase 'outer freedom' would perhaps be better vocabulary for the freedoms which arise for inter-human and inter-group relationships. 'Vocabulary' constitutes a real problem concerning many topics around religious liberty; so much so that we intend to publish someday some kind of 'dictionary' on questions of religious freedom.

consequences, than by restraining or coercing him in order to keep him from making mistakes. The second aspect of the same Christian insight is what we could call God's ways with men: God as disclosed in Jesus Christ is neither arbitrary nor coercive. It is an essential characteristic of the Gospel that God himself does not use force to win our allegiance. And this divine respect for human freedom is a revelation, directed decisively at the world, about the source and meaning of power, for even the State and its coercive power exists by virtue of the love and power of God, who does not compel faith.

For the theologians who are reluctant to accept the above-indicated essential interrelations between inner Christian freedom and social religious liberty the latter is rather the consequence of Christian teaching on the authority of worldly powers and the limits set to them. As one of them explains, 'from the Christian view the State has authority from God, not unlimited, but limited. The secular authority is not entitled to rule over the conscience of man. The government cares for peace and order, for economic and social welfare, but it is not the ruler over man's conscience. Therefore, Christian doctrine can demand from the State that it recognize the right of the Christian to exercise his religion freely.'

The theological development and study of all these different positions will be the matter of the following chapters.

2

THE 'STATUS' OF MAN ACCORDING
TO CHRISTIAN REVELATION

As WE said in the previous chapter, what we called 'God's ways with men' and the consideration of the 'status' of man as he has been created, redeemed and called by God, are all aspects of the same spirit of Christian revelation and, therefore, it would be wrong to consider them as two different and separate theological developments. Nevertheless, for methodological reasons, we must treat these two aspects consecutively, although never forgetting that they are intimately interlocked.

We think it would be useful, first of all, to sum up the main ecumenical statements on this matter.

'The Church knows—affirms the Oxford Conference—that man has been created in the image of God and has therefore an indestructible value.'[1]

Amsterdam stated: 'Man is created and called to be a free being, responsible to God and his neighbour. Any tendencies in State and Society depriving man of the possibility of acting responsibly are a denial of God's intention for man and his work of salvation.'[2]

In another report the same General Assembly said: 'Every person has a place in the divine purpose. Created by God in his image, the object of his redeeming love in Christ, he must be free to respond to God's calling.'[3]

The great Declaration on Religious Liberty of Amsterdam almost literally reproduced the terms of the Oxford Conference, proclaiming that 'the nature and destiny of man by virtue of his creation, redemption and calling, and man's activities in family, State and culture,

---

[1] The World Conference on Church, Community and State, Oxford, 1937, Report of the Section on Church and State.
[2] First Assembly of the WCC, Amsterdam, 1948, Report on 'The Church and the Disorder of Society'.
[3] First Assembly of the WCC, Amsterdam, 1948, Report on 'The Church and the International Disorder'.

establish limits beyond which the government cannot with impunity go'.[1]

'We acknowledge and confess that Jesus Christ, who has borne the curse of the Law in our stead, and has for us vanquished the forces of destruction, is our freedom. In him and through him, we are free for God and our brethren, free to live a life of gratitude and service to him.'[2]

Similarly, the Madras Conference stressed that it is of 'great importance that the Church should realize afresh the grounds of its claims to religious freedom. These are primarily the rights and obligations of men as children of God, and its own existence as the Body of Christ, in which the Head speaks to the members and through which he makes himself known to all men.'[3]

Amsterdam renewed this statement in part, saying 'that all men are equal in the sight of God and that the rights of man derive directly from their status as the children of God'.[4]

Finally, the Third Assembly has recently declared that 'Christians see religious liberty as a consequence of God's creative work of his redemption of man in Christ and his calling of men into his service.'[5]

We do not think we should ignore the fact that these ecumenical statements, owing to the necessary brevity of such documents and also perhaps to a certain 'apologetic complex',[6] are often somewhat vague and their terminology slightly imprecise and at times even incorrect. But we do think that their *substance* can be very useful for leading us in our study.

The Commission on Religious Liberty unanimously accepted the general formulation of this theological foundation, which it expressed as follows:

'God created man in his own image and redeemed him by his own free act of grace in Christ and calls him to a life of sonship in freedom, in which the responsibility to accept or reject is placed upon man himself.'[7]

The subsequent discussions within the Commission itself and the suggestions of several advisers resulted in another formulation

[1] First Assembly of the WCC, Amsterdam, 1948, Declaration on Religious Liberty; The World Conference on Church, Community and State, Oxford, 1937, Additional Report on 'Church and State'.
[2] Second Report of the Advisory Commission of the Second Assembly of the WCC.
[3] Conference on the World Mission of the Church, Madras, 1938.
[4] First Assembly of the WCC, Amsterdam, 1948, Report on 'The Church and the Disorder of Society'.
[5] Third Assembly of the WCC, New Delhi, 1961, Statement on Religious Liberty.
[6] See above, Introduction, pp. 11–12.
[7] Commission on Religious Liberty, Minutes of the Spittal Meeting, 1959.

in which two elements, namely God's love to men and the social impact of the God–man relationship, were particularly stressed:

> 'In love God created man in his image, in love he redeemed him in Jesus Christ, and in love he called him to be a free child of his in Christ; therefore each man is responsible in matters of religion solely before God. Nothing can basically alter this relation between God and man, but human coercion can and often does assault man's power to cling by faith to that relationship and, because it thus seeks to do violence to man's essential nature, it is sin.'[1]

Another aspect that the Commission has underlined is the Christological import of man's status in the light of the revelation:

> 'In Jesus Christ, God has both restored and redeemed his human creation, made in his own image. A particular man was and is the bearer of the fulness of God's majesty and purpose. In Jesus Christ he has called humanity to a destiny for the pursuit of which every man must be free. . . .'[2]

Among the comments made by several advisers and theologians on this particular topic of the 'status' of man[3] as it has been revealed by God, there is criticism of a general character. Some, indeed, think that the formulations of the ecumenical statements, as well as those of the Commission on this matter, are lacking in methodological cohesion and that they have not a 'compulsion' which would, by its theological clarity, be convincing. They suggest various formulations, for instance a trinitarian one, a *'heilsgeschichtliche'*, another grounded on the 'trinomium' faith-hope-love, or something similar. A distinguished Dutch theologian, Dr Berkhof,[4] proposes a trinitarian formulation which we will try to sum up as follows:

The Father created man in his own image. The Son has redeemed him and has incorporated humanity into himself, in the freedom from sin, from law and from death. The Spirit vivifies him with grace and gives him the faculty to call God 'Abba', Father, and of living the life of a child of God. The whole context, so to say, of the created, redeemed and called man is established

---

[1] Last Draft of 'A Christian Statement on the Nature and Basis of Religious Liberty' submitted to the Central Committee of the WCC, St Andrews, 1960.

[2] 'A Christian Statement', submitted to the Central Committee of the WCC, St Andrews, 1960.

[3] We intentionally avoid the term 'nature' of man which, of course, could be correctly interpreted, but which could also give occasion to a mistaken understanding in the sense of 'natural law' or of some rationalistic conception.

[4] Prof. Berkhof, Member of the Committee on Religious Liberty.

by the trinitarian God in terms of freedom. Free is the man
created in his own image by the most free Creator and Providence.
Free is the man redeemed and incorporated by Christ into a life of
grace and love, liberated from law and from fear. Free is the
man elevated by the Spirit to the dignity of the divine sonship and
to the law of love. Every relation of man to God, every action of
the divine Persons concerning humanity, contribute to set man,
the whole man, free in his individual as well as in his social context.

It is unfortunate that neither this nor other similar theological
development has so far been subjected to ecumenical discussion
and analysis.

Other comments on this matter refer to the analysis of the
different elements which constitute man's status in the light of
revelation.

There are some theologians who think that the element of
creation (together with the 're-creation' or redemption by Christ)
is of paramount importance. Thus, for instance, Wilder writes:

> 'The ultimate freedom of the creature, according to the New Testa-
> ment, is grounded first of all in *creation*. In generic terms we find
> this theme in Romans 1–2 and in Acts 14.[1] It is presented also in
> terms of the exemplary and representative role of Adam in Romans
> 5.12 ff., Phil. 2.6 and Acts 17.[2] This basic grounding is further ex-
> hibited and reinforced in the *covenant* relation to God in which the
> people of God and its members individually are seen as responsible
> to him, as those blessed by his prior acts of covenant-grace and call-
> ing. The "new" or renewed covenant and the *redemption* which
> establishes it reinforce the same immediacy and ultimacy of the
> creature's responsibility.'[3]

[1] Cf., for instance, Rom. 1.21: '. . . knowing God, they have refused to
honour him'; Rom. 2.5–6: 'you are laying up for yourself a store of retribution
for the day of retribution, when God's just judgment will be revealed, and he
will pay every man for what he has done'; Acts 14.15: 'The good news we bring
tells you to turn from these follies to the living God, who made heaven and
earth and sea and everything in them.'

[2] Cf. Rom. 5.12 and 15: 'It was through one man that sin entered the world,
and through sin death. . . . But God's act of grace is out of all proportion to
Adam's wrongdoing. For if the wrongdoing of that one man brought death
upon so many, its effect is vastly exceeded by the grace of God and the gift that
came to so many by the grace of the one man, Jesus Christ'; Phil. 2.5–7: 'Let
your bearing towards one another arise out of your life in Christ Jesus. For the
divine nature was his from the first; yet he did not think to snatch at equality
with God but made himself nothing, assuming the nature of a slave'; Acts
17.24–25: 'The God who created the world and everything in it, and who is
Lord of heaven and earth. . . . It is not because he lacks anything that he accepts
service at men's hands. . . .'

[3] Art. cit., p. 414.

This ultimate *responsibility* of the human creature before God is viewed by many theologians as one of the most fundamental elements of this aspect of revelation and that which more properly places the human status in its social context and man's responsibility in the frame of the divinely fixed destiny and vocation, not only on the individual but also on the social level of the different community activities in their proper functions, such as marriage, family, nation and culture.[1] It is in the context of this human responsibility that some advisers particularly consider man's capacity 'to see himself as a sinner, and to repent, which for the Christian is surely the beginning of wisdom, and which alone may save progress from disaster'.[2]

We must register very different reactions among ecumenical theologians to the consideration of man as '*imago Dei*' which we often find in the official statements. Some of them believe that 'the only Christian motive' for religious freedom is 'love for a being created in God's image'.[3] Consequently, the French Commission of Studies proposed the following formulation for this insight: 'Since every human being is created in the image of God and is called to benefit from the death and resurrection of Jesus Christ, he deserves to be respected, even when he makes mistakes.' Other theologians are much more reserved concerning this '*imago Dei*'. Far from considering it 'the only Christian motive' for religious liberty, Wilder thinks that 'the New Testament can hardly be said to identify the "*imago Dei*" with man's freedom. In Col. 3.10 the most we find is the idea that the new "man" or new humanity is "renewed unto *knowledge* after the image of God who created it".'[4] Others go much further and believe that the consideration of the '*imago Dei*' could serve both as a foundation for religious freedom and for the very denial of that freedom: 'If man is made in the image of God—they say—he is certainly committed to allowing that image to shine forth within him, but

[1] Cf. the World Conference on Church, Community and State, Oxford, 1937, Additional Report on 'Church and State'.

[2] Sir Kenneth Grubb (Chairman of the Commission of the Churches on International Affairs) in his suggestions to the Commission.

[3] Remarks of the 'Commission d'Etudes Oecuméniques', Fédération Protestante de France.

[4] Art. cit., p. 414. A modern translation of the text adduced from Col. 3.10, more in accordance with the original expression, says: '. . . the new nature, which is being constantly *renewed in the image of its Creator* and brought to know God' (The New English Bible). We see that the knowledge of God (and of his will) is here considered as a consequence of being man in God's image.

he may be equally committed to suppressing what he regards as a distortion of the image.'[1]

We dare not presume to give a definite judgment on this discussion, which we offer to the study of the churches. Nevertheless, we would like to make some observations which could perhaps throw some light on the reason why ecumenical bodies so often spoke of the '*imago Dei*' in the context of religious freedom. First of all we do not believe that this consideration should be produced 'as a piece of abstract theory', or as some logical argument extracted from the whole biblical ethos. The idea that man is the *imago Dei* and, therefore, man is free because God is the perfectly free Being, is an incorrect simplification of the matter. The *reality* of this 'image' is, in our opinion, much more complex. We are told that man is made in the image of God for he too is a spirit, because he is an intelligent being, endowed with the faculty to think, able to judge and to decide. It is, we think, this whole spiritual complex which constitutes man's divine '*similitudo*'. And it is again this whole spiritual complex which is the basis of man's individual *and* social freedom. At this point we consider particularly pertinent Luther's citation made by one of our best advisers. As '*imago Dei*', man is able to think, to have thoughts. And Luther says: 'For the proverb is true, "thoughts are free". Why then would they [the princes] constrain people to believe from the heart, when they see that it is impossible? In this way they compel weak consciences to lie, to deny, and to do what they do not believe in their hearts, and they load themselves down with dreadful alien sins.'[2] Luther's text clearly shows us, we think, not only that the reality of man as created '*ad similitudinem Dei*' demands freedom, internal and external, but also that this essential interrelation between both freedoms, of which we spoke,[3] is familiar to the best reformed tradition.

Similarly, in this whole theological and biblical context, we do not think that, in virtue of this '*imago Dei*', man 'may be equally committed to suppressing what he regards as a distortion of this image'. On the contrary, this image imperatively demands that

---

[1] Italian Commission on Religious Liberty.

[2] Luther, 'On Secular Authority', Holman edition of the *Works of Martin Luther*, vol. II, p. 254. Note also that, for Luther *the fact* of the psychological constraint which society (he speaks, of course, about 'princes') is able to exercise, justifies the claims for religious freedom. (See our ch. I of Part II, pp. 59–60.)

[3] Cf. above, Part II, ch. I, pp. 58–62.

man's spiritual ability of thinking, of judging and of deciding be fully respected. The opposite, according to Luther, would be to 'load ourselves with dreadful alien sins'.

In the opinion of various theologians, such expressions as the 'dignity of man' and 'child of God' also call for some reserve, at least concerning their interpretation. Thus, for instance, Wilder writes:

> 'Nor can one say that the "dignity" of man or the "rights" of man are taught in the New Testament as corollaries of his freedom. Such formulations may with caution be read into the Scripture but it should be recognized that they arise in the context of a later Christian anthropology and are easily exposed to misunderstanding. The dignity or rights or value of men as the children of God and as loved by him should be understood in the context of the Cross if they are to have their full significance and if we are to avoid a secularization leading either to banality or destructive illusions.'[1]

We should perhaps stress here two particular dangers of these 'destructive illusions'. The first one is to exaggerate this 'dignity' of man in such a manner as to make him wholly superior to society and independent from it. This is not the biblical idea of man's dignity and autonomy. Man is subjected, according to God's will and providence, to society, *although not wholly*. We think the following formulation by Thomas Aquinas on this matter is strikingly relevant: 'Man is not wholly subordinated to community, in everything he is and in everything he possesses; while he *is* subordinated to God in everything he is and in everything he possesses'.[2] This could also be a precious normative insight concerning religious liberty.

Another special danger is that of 'secularization' (to use Wilder's expression) of these insights. Professor Vittorio Subilia, in one of his outstanding communications, stressed this danger in a matter in which theological insights can easily be confused with humanistic and secular considerations, thus forming some kind of syncretistic synergism.[3]

As we said, the consideration of man's status as created,

---

[1] Art. cit., p. 414.   [2] *Summa Theologica* I–II, q. 21, a. 4, *ad* 3.
[3] 'Si les raisons théologiques de la liberté religieuse vont se fondre dans une espèce de synergisme avec les raisons non-théologiques, le fondement même de la liberté religieuse ne paraît plus être clair et sûr, et de toute manière ne peut plus s'inspirer à des raisons chrétiennes originelles.' Another quite different question is whether non-theological grounds can arrive at the same conclusions as the specifically Christian ones. We intend to study this problem elsewhere in this Part.

redeemed and called by God to an eternal destiny is a purely theological investigation, into which only specifically Christian principles should enter. And even this consideration is only one aspect of the general Christian insight concerning the essential God-man relationship, of which God's way with men is another aspect.

3

GOD'S WAYS WITH MEN

IN SHARP contrast to the insights exposed in the previous
chapter, the consideration of God's method in dealing with men,
at least in the form of a theological synthesis, has only been
recently included in ecumenical statements, so that we only have
two declarations (both definitely approved by the New Delhi
Assembly in 1961) which deal explicitly with this aspect of
Christian insights concerning religious freedom. We consider
both of great importance and worthy of being reproduced here:

'God's truth and love are given in freedom and call for a free response.
God does not coerce man to respond to his love; and the revelation
of God in Christ is a revelation that men are not forced to accept. He
calls men to make a willing and obedient response to him in faith, to
answer with a free and confident "yes" to the eternal action of his love
in which he reveals himself. This utterly free assent is undermined
and destroyed when human coercion enters in. Human coercion
denies the respect for every individual person which God's loving
action in Christ affirms. The non-coercive method and spirit of
Christ is in itself the condemnation of all attempts to force men's
religious beliefs or to purchase their allegiance, and for the Christian
it is the ground of religious liberty.'[1]

'God's redemptive dealing with men is not coercive. Accordingly,
human attempts by legal enactment or by pressure of social custom
to coerce or to eliminate faith are violations of the fundamental ways
of God with men. The freedom which God has given in Christ
implies a free response to God's love, and the responsibility to serve
fellow-men at the point of deepest need.'[2]

Even if ecumenical statements are not cited as a final response

[1] Third Assembly of the WCC, New Delhi, 1961, Report on 'Christian
Witness, Proselytism and Religious Liberty'. This Report had already been
received by the Central Committee at St Andrews, 1960, and transmitted to the
member churches for consideration and comment. Cf. *Minutes and Reports of
the Thirteenth Meeting of the Central Committee*, pp. 212–18.
[2] Third Assembly of the WCC, New Delhi, 1961, Statement on Religious
Liberty.

to the questions discussed, we think that these two declarations, both unanimously accepted by the Third Assembly, may throw light on our investigation.[1]

Both statements have their origin in the work and discussion of the Commission on Religious Liberty and in its efforts to find a general theological formulation which could include elements scattered in prior ecumenical declarations, as, for instance, the topics of Christian love, faith and obedience, which the theologians of the Commission considered as belonging together within the context of a superior theological synthesis.

The first formulation of this insight, made by the Commission at its Spittal Meeting, was much shorter, but already included, we think, all essential elements: 'God does not coerce men to respond to his love. The revelation of God in Christ is not a revelation which comes with exterior power. Christ rejected all forms of coercion, but humbled himself and came in the form of a servant.'[2]

If we are not mistaken, the essential and leading element of this insight is that *the act of God in Christ is the result of a free decision, the free giving of the Son, and therefore requires a free response.* The Christian Gospel primarily relates to the realm of freedom and provides the needed organizing principle in that realm. That principle is again human *responsibility* before God, which we have found already while considering man's status as it appears in the Christian revelation.

God, as disclosed in Jesus Christ, is neither arbitrary nor coercive. He has placed man in a world endowed with everything needful for his full development. Furthermore, God has given men freedom to use these gifts as they choose, and he respects their freedom even when they make bad use of it, though they have to take full responsibility for it.

The heart of the biblical revelation of God's love and concern for mankind is that in Jesus Christ he laid aside all divine glory in order to live among men in the form of a servant who humbled himself and in free obedience accepted even death—death on the cross.[3] To the acceptance of his revelation God leads us in Christ lovingly and invitingly, never forcing us: 'Behold, I stand at the

[1] Cf. above, Preface, p. 8.
[2] Minutes of the Spittal Meeting of the Commission on Religious Liberty, 1959.
[3] Cf. Phil. 2.8.

door, and knock: *if any man hear my voice, and open the door*, I will come into him, and will sup with him, and he with me.'[1]

It follows that man's religious acts can constitute an authentic response to God only when they are voluntary and uncoerced. No intellectual ingenuity, no organized institution, no kind of compulsion and no power of persuasion can change the fact that God deals with men as with free and responsible beings and that he expects from them an uncoerced response.

We think that in this essential and leading element of God's non-coercive method in dealing with men there is a general agreement, provided that it is correctly understood. We say provided that it is correctly understood, for this principle can be mistakenly and unnecessarily exaggerated in a sense alien both to Scripture and to theology.

First of all, while it is true that our Lord's self-revelation requires a free response, we should not forget that its proclamation is set in a biblical context which includes judgment and the possibility of eternal loss. As Bishop Newbigin pertinently indicates, in the Gospel there are also sayings concerning the man who causes one of these little ones to stumble, and the terrible words of Matthew 23: 'You snakes, you vipers' brood, how can you escape being condemned to hell?'[2]

Similarly, emphasis on man's freedom in responding to God's revelation should not let us forget the biblical teachings about the enslavement of man's will by sin and the mystery of election. Our Christian insight is neither 'semi-Pelagianism' nor Origen's optimism of the '*apokatasthasis pantón*'. But, on the other hand, it need not be. God's eschatological coercive authority, his final sanction and judgment, is perfectly compatible with his gracious persuasion: 'If thou willst have life eternal. . . .' Again, man's enslavement by sin and the mystery of his election by God does not impede the possibility of his freely accepting or refusing God's revelation. We find the confirmation of this compatibility in the same context of Matthew 23: 'How often *have I longed* to gather your children, as a hen gathers her brood under her wings; but *you would not let me*.'[3]

Another element that should be taken into account for a correct understanding of the non-coercive character of God's revelation is the actual existence of human coercion in the world. We

[1] Rev. 3.20.   [2] Matt. 23.33.   [3] Matt. 23.37.

Christians do not accept *dualism*. On the contrary, we believe, according to the Scriptures, that the existence (in the State, for example) of a realm in which coercion is used is God's will and, in its final purpose, for the service of God. The Bible teaches us to believe that this realm, in which coercion is employed, is also ordained by God. Now, as Bishop Newbigin[1] says, 'the deep perplexity arises when these two facts seem to lead to opposite conclusions'. If the whole Gospel and the teaching of Jesus on the Kingdom of God 'breathes' freedom, to use Vinet's expression, how can we explain this human coerciveness which is ordained by God? And, above all, where does religious liberty stand in the struggle between these two apparently opposite elements?

We must confess that neither of the categories of traditional theology throw much light on this problem, nor do modern thinkers do much work in opening up fresh areas of inquiry. One of our advisers rightly wonders whether it would not be useful and necessary to investigate this matter on the line of the following questions:

> To what extent does God's non-coercive action imply a judgment on the coercive elements of human society and any other coercion in the relations of man to man?
>
> Does the New Testament exposition of law and grace provide an understanding of human coerciveness and a way of dealing with it?
>
> How is the emergence of non-coercive organs of social and political action (e.g. the United Nations and its agencies, the WCC, etc.) related to the Christian understanding of man as being created for freedom?
>
> Does the New Testament teach or imply that the Church is essentially a non-coercive society? Is it intended to be the prototype of civil society generally in this respect?
>
> How does the teaching of Jesus on the Kingdom of God bear on these questions?
>
> How does our Lord's suffering and triumph bear on these questions?

We indeed think that a study oriented on this line could be extremely helpful for clarifying this problem, and we very much hope that churches and their theologians may take an active part in this investigation which, alas, is still at its very beginning.

We should perhaps let this important problem rest here, with all its questions open, and simply wait for pertinent answers.

---

[1] Bishop Lesslie Newbigin, former General Secretary of the International Missionary Council, Assistant General Secretary of the WCC.

Nevertheless, we would like to make our little contribution, although we are well aware of its incompleteness.

The 'non-coerciveness' of God's revelation as well as human coercion in the civil society have been ordained by God. This coexistence must necessarily occasion tensions and struggles, and both Bible and history give us witness of them.

The distinction of the 'two realms', of the 'eternal' and the 'temporal' order, of the things which are God's and those which are Caesar's, is, of course, correct but, as we shall see later,[1] it is not sufficient to solve our problem. In fact, too many things are *in part eternal* and *in part temporal* to find complete satisfaction in such a distinction. Ecumenical insights recognize both that the Church has the right and the duty to proclaim the implications of its religious beliefs for social, economic and political relationships, and that the civil society may not be wholly indifferent to religion.

Nevertheless, although we also recognize the impossibility of perfectly distinguishing between the two realms indicated above because of the historical and necessary interrelation of the two, *the principle holds* that men have higher loyalties than those which they have to society and State; the principle holds that, among those higher loyalties, the highest ones are those which make man responsible solely before God, namely the religious loyalties; the principle holds that the destiny of man and the divine purpose for him 'constitute an irremovable limit of the State which it cannot with impunity transgress'.[2]

Unfortunately, theological investigation has not, so far, satisfactorily clarified the dynamic interaction between God's non-coercive revelation and the coercive elements of human society, nor the judgment which is perhaps implied in the priority of the former. Still less clear are the exact boundaries of this 'irremovable limit' of the State's competence, and we even wonder whether such precise delimitation can be formulated merely in view of theological principles without consideration of the factual circumstances of each concrete civil society in time, space and culture. But we think that this uncertainty and hesitancy only shows that the practical harmony between necessary freedom and some no less necessary human coercion must be looked for through the con-

[1] See below, Part III, ch. 4, 'Responsible State', pp. 124–134.
[2] The World Conference on Church, Community and State, Oxford, 1937, Additional Report on 'Church and State'.

sideration of concrete circumstances but always under the leader-
ship of our superior Christian insights.

As we said above, the general insight of God's method in dealing
with men includes various topics which have been treated
separately by ecumenical bodies and whose consideration may be
useful for the complete understanding of the divine ways with
humanity.

These topics are mainly three: Faith, Obedience and Love.
Considering that Christian obedience, man's loyalty to God, is
essentially based on the unconditional trust of man and on his sure
hope that God will fulfil his promises,[1] we think it possible to treat
this matter within the 'trinominal' composition, suggested by Dr
Berkhof, of Faith-Hope-Love.

The term *'faith'* is not taken here in the analogical sense of the
contents of faith, or of the revealed truths which are the object of
faith, but in the sense of the virtue by which man accepts divine
revelation. And we say that 'the revelation of God in Christ is a
revelation that men are not forced to accept. God calls men to
make a willing and obedient response to him in faith, to answer
with a free and confident "yes" to the eternal action of his love in
which he reveals himself.'[2]

We affirm then that our Christian faith is an 'utterly free assent'.[3]
Nevertheless, our affirmation by no means coincides with the
humanist concept of freedom in the simple sense of 'natural free
will', nor with the semi-Pelagianist conception of faith as a product
of the free and *independent* exercise of human faculties. On the
contrary:

(a) Faith is God's gift. Man cannot come to the Father in faith unless
it is given unto him by the Spirit.

(b) Faith is not the consequence of the proclamation of a logical
truth which can compel recognition by the intellect. As Dr
Visser 't Hooft[4] suggested, 'We believe by faith and not by sight.
God does not give us rational or mathematical proofs.'[5] Far from
this, 'salvation is offered to men in the highly paradoxical message

[1] Cf. for instance John 14.15–16: 'If you love me you will obey my commands;
and I will ask the Father, and he will give you another to be your Advocate, who
will be with you for ever, the Spirit of truth.'
[2] Third Assembly of the WCC, New Delhi, 1961, Report on 'Christian
Witness, Proselytism and Religious Liberty'.
[3] *Ibid.*   [4] Dr Visser 't Hooft, General Secretary of the WCC.
[5] Minutes of the Spittal Meeting of the Commission on Religious Liberty
1959.

of the Word made flesh and crucified, in a *"theologia crucis"* in which the evidence of God's love is concealed *"sub contraria specie"*, to take over an expression of Luther. There is thus a kind of non-evidence inherent in the paradoxical nature of the Gospel that cannot be eliminated without thereby changing the very nature of faith, which is *a choice of the soul, a decision, a risk* to take.'[1]

We are well aware, and ecumenical bodies are too, that this free and voluntary choice, this valiant confidence which trusts in God's truth, primarily concerns our inner Christian freedom which cannot be humanly created nor destroyed. But we also know that our capacities for free and conscious choice can be cruelly crushed by external coercion, even though any compulsion man would apply to his fellow-men must necessarily fail to reach that which is deepest in his nature—his relation to God which cannot be other than free. Thus it would appear that coercion is something completely alien and strange to the essence of the Christian faith and does not operate, so to say, on the same dimension. It is in this sense of total disproportion and essential opposition that we say faith 'is undermined and destroyed when human coercion enters in'.[2]

Christian *hope* in the fulfilment of God's promise has also a clear bearing on religious liberty. Hope means both expectation and confidence. The expectation of eternal life necessarily implies the freedom to follow on earth the divine calling and of walking 'in the paths of justice' as God and our own conscience prescribe. Moreover, hope, in the sense of confidence, leads us to that trustful 'yes' to the eternal action of God's love,[3] which is the essence of Christian obedience. As it has been declared, 'The Christian revelation, as contained in Holy Scripture,[4] lays upon every man the basic demand that he should first and foremost obey God and consequently requires of all others that they should in no way circumscribe this obedience'.[5]

Man is liberated in Jesus Christ in order that he may live a life of obedience to God. In the freedom to which God has called him,

[1] Cf. Suggestions of the Italian Commission on Religious Liberty.
[2] Third Assembly of the WCC, New Delhi, 1961, Report on 'Christian Witness, Proselytism and Religious Liberty'.
[3] Cf. Third Assembly of the WCC, New Delhi, 1961, *ibid.*
[4] Cf. Acts 5.29: 'Peter replied for himself and the apostles: "We must obey God rather than men".'
[5] Conference of the Protestant Churches of the Latin European Countries, Chambon-sur-Lignon, 1958, 'Resolutions on Religious Liberty'.

man is invited to become God's fellow-worker in the fulfilment of this obedience. There is, then, in our due Christian obedience, a relationship between God and man which is based on freedom. This carries with it the obligation on each man's part to obey God himself and consequently in no way to prevent or hinder the obedience of others, privately or publicly. To be true to the human dignity bestowed by God, man must above all be loyal to him, and it needs to be recognized that this loyalty must transcend his loyalty to family, society and nation.

No man or human institution, however, can, with ultimate authority, define the will of God or enforce obedience to it. The very existence of such an unconditional obligation upon man implies that each man must be free to seek out and to follow God's will as he sees it.[1] Therefore, Christians oppose 'any attempt to impair the freedom of men to obey God and to act according to conscience'.[2]

At the same time, however, we must affirm that Christians are called to offer ultimate obedience to God alone in whom they solely trust, whatever may be the consequences to them even of acting against unjust legal provisions, for we know, both from the Scriptures and from experience, that the State may become an instrument of evil. 'Every Christian'—concludes the New Delhi Assembly—'has the liberty individually or in the corporate body of a church or other group to put his whole existence under the authority of God, to believe, pray, worship and proclaim Christ, as well as to live in accordance with his will, in the church of his choice.'[3]

A particular but very important case of this trustful Christian obedience is constituted by our duty to proclaim the Gospel in accordance with the Lord's commandment: 'Full authority in heaven and on earth has been committed to me. Go forth therefore and make all nations my disciples.'[4] God's gracious action towards

[1] See what has been said above on problems of conscience, Part I, ch. 3, pp. 20–26.
[2] First Assembly of the WCC, Amsterdam, 1948, Report on 'The Church and the Disorder of Society'.
[3] Third Assembly of the WCC, New Delhi, 1961, Report on 'Christian Witness, Proselytism and Religious Liberty'. Cf. also the First Assembly of the WCC, Amsterdam, 1948, Report on 'The Church and the International Disorder': 'The Church has always demanded freedom to obey God rather than men. . . . [The churches] must work for an ever wider and deeper understanding of what are the essential human rights if men are to be free to do the Will of God.'
[4] Matt. 28.18 f.

us, in which we are called to the free obedience of the sons of God, invites us to preach the Gospel to all men. Therefore, the Church claims freedom to bear this witness in human society, because its duty is to speak of that on which the being of man and of human community is based. 'Every Christian church is not only permitted but required freely and openly to bear witness in the world, seeking to bring persons into fellowship with God as revealed in Jesus Christ.'[1] Moreover, Christians must eschew the use of any kind of force while propagating their faith. Coercion for winning religious allegiance implies the contradiction of God's ways with men as well as a lack of trust in the power of the Holy Spirit and putting our hope elsewhere than on God's Lordship and on the strength of his grace. In particular, we must be on our guard against any ecclesiastical institutions which seek to avail themselves of political power to enforce religious uniformity, or to claim for their own advantage any compulsion which may be exercised by civil authorities.

Thirdly, 'God's *love* is given in freedom and calls for a free response';[2] 'the freedom which God has given in Christ implies a free response to God's love'.[3] Our Gospel is essentially a Gospel of love: 'for in Jesus Christ neither circumcision availeth anything, nor uncircumcision; but faith which worketh by love.'[4] Through God's redeeming love in Christ man is liberated from the bondage of fear and drawn to God by love. This paradoxically liberating subjection by love was doubtless meant by Jesus when he said: 'And I, if I be lifted up from the earth, will draw all men unto me.'[5] Not by fear, but by grace; not by dominating power, but by loving sacrifice on the cross, which can only be satisfied with responding love.

God, then, by his redemption, gives love and expects love: 'As the Father hath loved me, so have I loved you: continue ye in my love.'[6] In return for the supreme gift of love which he has given of himself, God demands the free gift of man's love. For complete liberty exists only where man is not under the compulsion of a law but under the influence of charity: 'If ye keep my command-

---

[1] The Third Assembly of the WCC, New Delhi, 1961, *ibid.*
[2] Third Assembly of the WCC, New Delhi, 1961, Report on 'Christian Witness, Proselytism and Religious Liberty'.
[3] Third Assembly of the WCC, New Delhi, 1961, Statement on Religious Liberty.
[4] Gal. 5.6.   [5] John 12.32.   [6] John 15.9.

ments, ye shall abide in my love; even as I have kept my Father's commandments, and abide in his love.'[1] It is this free homage that God claims, for it is only then that man gives himself.

Christians therefore, if they be true to evangelical teaching, have no temptation to evade this fundamental 'law' of free love, neither for themselves nor for others. Moreover, the commandment to love our neighbours, being similar to that to love God, also makes Christians, in virtue of this same charity, respect the religious freedom of others as well as their desire to be free themselves.

Love and grace liberate us from the compulsion of the law. This clarifies still more God's redemptive attitude towards men. Paul perceived that law and grace are essentially different, even antithetic, because they involve radically different ways of dealing with the needs of man and society. 'Law', says Dr Carpenter,[2] 'is the pattern in which man makes as little return as he can to God (and to society) for what he has received; grace is the pattern in which he gives all he has out of sheer gratitude. Law is coercive and gives rise to evasion, irresponsibility and estrangement; grace is non-coercive, healing and reconciling.' In one short word, the law operates in the realm of social constraint, whilst the work of Christ was to free us from this tyranny and to transfer us to the realm of freedom and grace. So the Christian, who has become spiritually free through faith in Christ 'which worketh by love', must always be concerned about respecting the freedom of others and making freedom, rather than coercion, the operative principle of human relations.

Christian faith, hope and love, then, show us still more clearly that God's redemptive ways with men presuppose freedom and demand freedom; firstly, of course, personal and inner freedom, but also that social freedom which sets the whole human community on the tracks of the world's divine redemption. Some theologians doubt whether these three graces in Christian experience (faith, hope, love) can be separated from one another, or whether they can be separately related to the experience of freedom. We feel, however, that those who suggested this kind of theological analysis by no means meant to separate these graces *in real Christian life*, but only to analyse them systematically. As is well known, analysis often involves some *conceptual* separation of things which are really united. Besides, it seems obvious that

---

[1] John 15.10.　　　　　　[2] Dr Carpenter, officer of the IMC.

human experience in the exercise of the Christian virtues of faith, hope and love is but *a part* of the free response to God's calling which has been explained in this chapter, and which does not constitute a substantially different approach to the theological grounds for religious liberty.[1]

Before closing this chapter we would like to stress that in our opinion the two aspects which we studied in the two last chapters, namely that the revelation of God's love in dealing with mankind requires a free response and that the status of man as revealed by God is that of free responsibility, join and complete each other in one and the same reality or theological 'complex'. God's redemptive dealing with men has not only left them free to accept the divine revelation but, precisely by virtue of this non-coercive method and providence, God has made, redeemed and called man to be freely responsible before himself and before his fellow-men.

[1] At this point, some advisers suggested that while the first of the factors of God's non-coercive method is obviously God's love for mankind, the second could be God's recognition for the demands of justice on man's behalf. From the identification and interrelation of these two factors would emerge, according to these advisers, the following:

(a) a standard of non-coercive methods toward which man and all organs of society should strive;

(b) a measure of man's capacity and performance which gives a clue to the problems and limitations upon religious liberty primarily because man is not God and, whether because of weakness or sin, cannot reproduce in experience the two fundamentals which underlie God's non-coercive method;

(c) a suggestion as to the procedure for meeting the problems and moving toward a standard for non-coercive methods.

We shall return to part of these suggestions when dealing, in Part III, with the problems of the responsible exercise of religious liberty.

4

FRONTIERS OF THE STATE'S COMPETENCE

WE NOTED in a previous chapter[1] that, for some theologians, mainly German and Italian, religious liberty is founded rather on the Christian teaching of the authority of worldly powers and the limits set to them.

Ecumenical statements frequently stressed these limitations, proclaiming that 'it is presumptuous for the State to assume that it can grant or deny fundamental rights',[2] and that liberty, particularly religious liberty, 'is not a favour granted by some human authority'.[3]

Nevertheless, in all these declarations the limits of the State's power appear *as a consequence* of the fundamental Christian insights which we have studied in the two previous chapters. It is 'the nature and destiny of man by virtue of his creation, redemption and calling' which 'establish limits beyond which the government cannot with impunity go'.[4] It is because 'man has been created in the image of God and has therefore an indestructible value'; and because of 'God's intention for man' that he should act responsibly, that the State has not the right to impair religious liberty.[5]

On the contrary, for the other theologians the limitation on the

---

[1] See above, Part II, ch. 1, p. 63.
[2] First Assembly of the WCC, Amsterdam, 1948, Report on 'The Church and the International Disorder'.
[3] Declaration of the First Evangelical Conference of Latin America, Buenos Aires, 1949.
[4] First Assembly of the WCC, Amsterdam, 1948, Declaration on Religious Liberty. Cf. also: The World Conference on Church, Community and State, Oxford, 1937, Additional Report on 'Church and State'.
[5] The World Conference on Church, Community and State, Oxford, 1937, *ibid.*; First Assembly of the WCC, Amsterdam, 1948, Report on 'The Church and the Disorder of Society'. We shall study these limits in Part III, ch. 4, 'Responsible State'.

rights of political powers need not be deduced from the above indicated insights, but is in itself the only basis for religious liberty. We reproduce here the suggestions of one of our advisers:

'(a) The term "liberty" concerns the Christian in several ways. First of all it means Christian liberty as proclaimed by the Churches of the Reformation, i.e. *libertas christiana*. The Christian is free to obey God, free from all exterior power and force. This freedom springs from his faith and makes him free against all secular authority. It is his duty to follow the call, his also the freedom to do so without regard to worldly laws and demands. Christian freedom in this sense includes also the obligation to stand by his faith, to bear witness, even in dangerous circumstances and, finally, to be prepared even to suffer for his faith. This freedom is not proclaimed or recognized by secular powers, it is the inner gift of the Christian given him by God's grace.

'(b) The liberty of religious exercise in a State *flows from quite another source*.[1] *It must be derived from the limitation of political power*. From the Christian view the State has but limited, not unlimited, authority from God. Secular authority is not entitled to rule over man's conscience. The government concerns itself with peace and order, with economic and social welfare, but it does not rule over man's conscience. Therefore Christian doctrine can demand from the State that it recognize the right to exercise one's religion freely. From a secular point of view, the same result can be won from the idea of human rights, of inborn or natural rights of the individual. They appear as limitations upon political power and as a guarantee against inroads of the State in the sphere of individual freedom.

'(c) For the Christian religious tolerance originates from two reasons: First, it has always been recognized that everybody should follow the call of Christ from his own conviction and not from fear or force. Second, Christian love demands it from every Christian, especially if he lives among heathen or—as is the case in all "Christian" countries of Europe—among people who call themselves Christian but who are Christian by name only. Tolerance cannot be derived from faith, because the Christian faith is absolute truth. Every inclination towards a recognition of "two or more possibilities of truth" must be avoided. Christian truth may never be a relative one. Therefore the Christian cannot demand freedom of religious opinion out of any doubt about the sole revelation of Christian faith, but only out of a sense of love towards all fellow-men and a sense of responsibility as a citizen who demands freedom of conscience from the State. The State's limitations, the principle that political power should not

[1] Our italics.

constrain conscience, is not to be derived from the free response of the Christian, but from the inherent limitation of political power.'

These suggestions contain many enlightening insights which would certainly be agreed on by all ecumenical thinkers and which coincide with various opinions explained in previous chapters. For this very reason we think it more useful to analyse carefully where this insight agrees with the convictions of the majority of theologians and where precisely it diverges from them.

To begin with, we think that everybody would agree on the conceptual distinction between social religious liberty and the '*libertas christiana*' or specific Christian liberty, although there are different opinions about their interrelations.[1] Nevertheless, some expressions concerning this distinction would perhaps not be accepted by all, at least not without some clear explanation. First of all, social religious liberty, in the opinion of many, should not be simply called 'a right in the State', but rather a social faculty which culminates in a civil right, in the sense that *also* to be a right is an attribute of this freedom, while its *essence* is to be a social faculty, which is a larger concept.[2]

Secondly, some would find it very difficult to accept the confusion between 'liberty' and 'obligation' which seems to be implied in phrases such as: 'Christian freedom . . . includes also the obligation to stand by his faith; . . . his [man's] is the duty to follow the call. . . .' It would appear that every liberty is essentially a *faculty*, some positive liberation '*a vinculo*'. Now, every obligation, every duty is a '*vinculum*' and, consequently, exactly the contrary of liberty. Of course, duty and freedom may be inter-related or even complete each other, perhaps the one can be the reason and foundation of the other. This shows that we may *relate* both concepts, but not *identify* them.

It would be still more difficult for many to accept, without explanation or distinction, the expression that Christian liberty makes man free 'against all secular authority'; 'without regard for worldly laws and demands'. Surely, such formulations can have a correct interpretation in the sense that the very concept of the '*libertas christiana*' does not say anything in itself about external

[1] See above, Part I, ch. 1, p. 17 f.
[2] See above, Part I, ch. 2, p. 21; similarly, Part I, ch. 4, p. 33 and the whole chapter.

liberty or external coercion, for it is an *inner* freedom which is conceptually independent from the external world. It is also correct that we have or can have the possibility of remaining internally free, by virtue of Christian liberty, whether we have or have not external freedom or the possibility of demanding it. But many would not like to formulate these assertions by saying that this freedom is against secular authority and without regard for worldly laws, for Christians, because of the virtue of freedom given by Christ, are *not* so absolutely independent from all secular authority, and they should have much regard, *as Christians*, for worldly laws when they are legitimate and just. In the very moment that the relation God–man (the giving by God of inner Christian freedom) originates a different relation of man to man (independence of man from secular authorities), the resulting situation must be regulated by the Christian insights concerning social and civil life and never forget the Christian duty proclaimed by Paul: 'Every person must submit to the supreme authorities'.[1] We wonder whether this confusion has not its source in an exaggerated *separation* (rather than *distinction*) between inner and social freedom, and in the mistaken 'dichotomy' of the individual and the social Christian of which we have already spoken.[2]

Having made these clarifications, we should now investigate the opinion that social religious liberty 'must be derived from the limitation of political power' and not 'from the free response of the Christian'.

Here we must make the observation that we made previously: for some theologians, even in a case in which this argument would be conclusive concerning the juridical right of religious liberty before the State, it would not cover the general faculty of liberation from *any kind of social compulsion* and, therefore, could not supply a basis for the *whole* social religious liberty as understood by those theologians.

Although everybody would subscribe to the assertion that the State has not unlimited but limited authority from God, and that the secular authority is not entitled to rule over the conscience of man, we do not think that the view that the State 'cares for peace and order, for economic and social welfare' would receive the same general approbation, for many ecumenical theologians

[1] Rom. 13.1.   [2] See above, Part I, ch. 1, p. 18.

believe that the common good of the civil community, which it is the State's duty to care for, includes other and larger areas.[1]

Similarly, it is generally admitted that the non-competence of the State over man's conscience is *a Christian view*, although it is certainly not an explicitly revealed truth. The precise question, however, is to know on what theological insight Christians base their view that this non-competence should *particularly apply to the affairs of man's conscience*. This is the central question on which opinions are clearly divided. The majority of theologians would, we think, argue in a manner similar to this: The Christian basis of the assertion that the State has no authority over man's conscience must be found either in the Christian revelation about the nature and functions of the State, or in the Christian revelation about man's status and God's ways with him. Now, it seems that it would be extremely difficult to find in the Christian revelation the precise limits of civil authority concerning man *in virtue of the State's nature*. On the contrary, Christian revelation does show us that man, as he has been created, redeemed and called by God and as God intends to deal with him, is responsible solely to God and that, *therefore*, the State, which is subordinated to God's authority and laws, must respect this human responsibility before God. Consequently, in thinking this way, religious liberty would *not* be ultimately based on the limitation of political authority but, inversely, the latter would flow from the freedom which God has given man.

Theologians who hold this opinion will not fail to remark that, in the text reproduced above, it is recognized that 'from a secular opinion, the same result [that government is not the ruler over man's conscience] can be won from the idea of human rights, of inborn or natural rights of the individual', so that 'they appear as limitations upon political power and as a guarantee against inroads of the State in the sphere of individual freedom'. It seems to them rather dubious to argue that, while for secular opinion limitations of political power are the consequence of man's freedom, for Christians man's freedom has to be the consequence of limitations of political power. . . . It is surely obvious that secular and Christian considerations can and often do follow very different ways but, in this particular case, many may wonder

---

[1] See above, Part II, ch. 3, pp. 74–77, and below, Part III, ch. 4, 'Responsible State'.

why secular reasoning and Christian insights should oppose each
other in such irreducible terms.

One of the reasons which lead some theologians to look for the
Christian basis of religious liberty in the limitations of civil power
is their reluctance to accept the view that religious freedom can be
derived from faith. As they say, 'tolerance cannot be derived from
faith, because the Christian faith is absolute truth.'

One wonders, however, whether this reluctance did not originate
from the ambiguity of the word 'faith'. Every Christian would
agree with the opinion that every inclination towards a recognition
of two or more possibilities of truth must be avoided and that,
therefore, we cannot demand freedom of religion based on our
religious doubts. Moreover, we deem it necessary to recall the
absoluteness of Christian truth understood as a living relatedness
reflecting the idea which Christ expressed as 'I am the truth.'
Every social religious liberty based on relativism of the truth or
on practical indifference concerning it is not a religious freedom
to be asked for by Christians. The consideration of the weakness
and fallibility of human thought (which should be accepted, if
correctly understood) can be the motivation for some individual
or social 'tolerance' towards the errors or mistakes of others; but
this should never be the theological basis for the complete social
liberty of all religions, as if all (including the Christian one) were
more or less equivalent concerning the revelation of the divine
truth. This would be syncretism or relativism; never Christian
insight.

But the formulation 'religious freedom based on faith' can have
another quite different meaning. For the term 'faith' is still more
equivocal than the expression 'religious liberty'. In theology (not
to speak of ordinary speech) it is employed in many different ways.
To give only a few examples, faith can mean 'revelation', i.e. the
divine truth which is the object and content of faith. Also called
faith is God's gift by which man is able to accept and to adhere to
the divine revealed truth. Faith is also correctly called the act of
believing what God has revealed to us, and even the internal
process whereby we cling to the revealed truth. Faith is also the
total Christian attitude by which the Christian not only believes
the divine truths but adheres to, trusts and loves the loving,
revealing God and lives according to his truth and will.

Consequently, the assertion that social religious liberty cannot be derived from 'faith' which is 'absolute truth' is perfectly correct if we mean by faith the revelation or the divine truths which are the content of revelation. But on the other hand this assertion cannot be applied to faith which is considered as a gift of God or as the act by which man, through Christ's grace, adheres and confides in God's revelation. These meanings do not directly concern the divine truths and, therefore, it is possible to base religious liberty on faith in this sense without falling into relativism. This, we think, was clearly explained when we treated the topics of Faith—Hope—Love as theological foundations for religious liberty.[1]

There is a final consideration which we think useful, not because of its controversial import but because it can lead to a greater clarification of the nature and basis of social religious liberty. We refer to the problems posed by the use of the term 'tolerance' as equivalent to religious freedom, while investigating the theological foundations of the latter.

We must register our view that 'tolerance' is again another very equivocal word. This ambiguity is so great that in some cases it is used even in a sense of opposition to or, at least, a limitation of religious liberty as, for instance, when it is said that Protestants are *tolerated* in Spain, by which is meant a restricted and discriminating permission. In the best meaning of the term, 'tolerance' expresses the moral attitude and also the moral duty of respecting opinions different from or opposite to our own insights. It seems obvious, therefore, that tolerance may be the moral motivation which can lead people to recognize and respect the religious freedom of others, but in no way is it the same thing as religious liberty itself.

Furthermore, tolerance, in this sense, moves on a different level from religious liberty, namely in a moral sphere. Religious freedom—social religious freedom—may have theological and moral motivations, but its sphere of exercise is a resolutely social and juridical one.

It is perhaps from this confusion that the opinion emerges that Christian love demands tolerance (= religious freedom) from every Christian. We have already indicated the correct way, in the opinion of many theologians, of basing religious liberty on

[1] See above, Part II, ch. 3, pp. 77–82.

Love.[1] But, on the other hand, it would seem that Christian love demands this respect for religious activities only if and when this human faculty, in the social context, has already been recognized, as well as its independence from human interference. Christian love does not command respect for all possible human activities: it does not command respect for murder, for arson, for adultery. Christian love commands respect for human activities *which are legitimate in themselves* and *which man has the right to perform in freedom from external coercion*. Now, how do we know that religious liberty concerns these particular kinds of human activities? Is it not because God made, redeemed and called man to an eternal destiny in which he should be essentially free, and because God, in his dealing with men, fully respects this freedom? Therefore, it would seem that Christian love is not the basis of religious freedom, *independently* from any other theological insight. Note that even the Golden Rule is not an exception to this, for it presupposes that *we* already have the faculty that we, *therefore*, should also recognize in others.

Where this minority opinion joins the great current of the ecumenical thinkers is when it says that 'it has always been recognized that everybody should follow the call of Christ from his own conviction and not from fear or force'. It is generally acknowledged that it is in the investigating of the reason for this assertion that opinions divide. For the great majority of the theologians, the ultimate reason for this is the revealed attitude of God towards men, as well in his creation, redemption and calling as in his redemptive dealings with humanity.

[1] See above, Part II, ch. 3, pp. 80–81.

5

THE PROBLEM OF AN UNDERSTANDING BETWEEN CHRISTIANS AND NON-CHRISTIANS ABOUT THE BASIS OF RELIGIOUS FREEDOM

THE PROBLEM posed in this chapter is briefly and clearly indicated in the following paragraph of a paper on 'Main Problems Concerning the Understanding of Religious Liberty' which was submitted to the consideration of our advisers:

> 'As the discussion proceeds, to what degree do considerations come forward which, although commendable, are not necessarily Christian in the sense that they may be used by non-Christians as well? Is it legitimate to include these considerations, for instance of a social or a juridical or a philosophical nature, in a total Christian apologia for religious liberty? If so, what connection is required between these arguments and those of a specifically theological nature? Upon what specific arguments for religious liberty can Christians make common cause with non-Christians?'

There is, in fact, very little agreement among ecumenical theologians on this argument.

However, two opinions are generally accepted by all. First, there is unanimous opposition against supporting religious freedom on grounds that we, as Christians, would disown, and which would rightly be called 'anti-Christian' grounds. These grounds would be, for instance, indifference, syncretism, tolerance at the price of compromised witness, and opportunism in accepting every religion as a method for opposing, say, Marxist atheism, etc. In the face of these insights which deny fundamental Christian convictions, and in consideration of the spreading of some of these wrong attitudes, every ecumenical theologian thinks that we should definitely safeguard our Christian position against misunderstanding from that side. Even expressions such as 'God's truth never becomes totally our possession', which are completely correct if correctly understood, should be avoided in a context which can give the impression of the *objective* relativism of the divine revelation.

We find another point of consensus in the opinion that, even if we may use specifically non-Christian considerations, we should never *mix* them with our theological insights. By 'mixing' arguments we understand the evolving of them in such a fashion that we *confuse* the theological and the philosophical issues, incorrectly passing from one to another or making incorrect deductions from one sphere of thinking to the other. In spite of this, it would not appear to be 'mixing arguments' to relate them or to investigate their eventual parallelism. For instance, if we discover the supreme worth of man in God's revelation while secular thinkers discover it in psychological and historical experience, we may well invest- igate whether both arguments really lead to the same conclusions in the same sense of the terms, and whether the premises and conclusions of rational arguments are philosophically correct.

Where the diversity of opinion is greatest is on the question of theoretical and historical import of the specifically non-Christian grounds and of the advisability of Christians using them.

A minority group in Latin America even feels that it is not necessary to insist on Christian grounds for religious liberty. First, because a specific Christian argument is not of 'universal value' for all men and, secondly, because the recognition of religious freedom has been historically won through the effort of liberal forces rather than on specifically Christian foundations. This minority does not think it unbecoming for Christians to believe or to do certain things just for the sake of human personality, because of our acknowledgment of some inherent rights embedded in the very self of man since his creation that prompts us to respect man's freedom to believe or not to practise his own type of obedience while we practise our Christian obedience.

The majority think, of course, that we should base religious liberty on specific Christian convictions and that we should by no means weaken the Christian witness which has certainly some- thing, and very important at that, to say on this matter. However, many within this majority believe that Christians should frankly recognize that some of the best contributions in favour of religious freedom have been made by thinkers outside the formal churches and even outside Christendom, and that opponents and critics of the Church have sometimes been the first to proclaim the liberty which should have been the glory of the Church to defend and promote. Christians, instead of boasting about their 'insights', should, in the opinion of these theologians, acknowledge with gratitude to God in humble confession the fact that God has raised other forces to do with heroic effort his work, while the churches were slow in understanding the consequences of the Christian revelation in this area.

Others, while recognizing a fragmentary truth in these considerations, are nevertheless of the opinion that they are somewhat exaggerated and that they neglect the long story which precedes the French philosophers. Dr Carlson,[1] for example, observes:

'The New Testament has persistently presented an emphasis on man's responsibility under God for his institutions and his spiritual response. Furthermore, a number of movements have a long history of special witness on the point. In the last analysis, the enlightenment combined a number of borrowed concepts, some of which had strong Christian roots. I believe it is important that the churches strengthen rather than weaken the Christian roots of freedom. Accordingly, we must face the issue of our generation standing not on transitory historical movements, but on the abiding religious insights of our faith. Our commitment must be at that high level. All of this neither erodes nor weakens our appreciation for those valid positions which have been taken by some social reformers, nor does it make us reluctant to co-operate with persons who believe in freedom but on different premises.'

This emphasis on our Christian insights, which does not exclude co-operation with non-Christians for the same purpose, should find an unrivalled opportunity for development at a time when we are experiencing a renaissance both in the depth and in the unity of our understanding of the Bible. There is today a unique opportunity for us to think together profoundly about what God's work in our Lord Jesus Christ ultimately implies for freedom, and to commend the result of our reflections not only to our fellow Christians but to all our fellow human beings.

Now we have established in the above text that the majority agree that we as Christians should particularly stress our specific Christian arguments grounded on Christian revelation, but the

[1] Dr C. Emanuel Carlson, Executive Director of the Baptist Joint Committee on Public Affairs (U.S.A.), member of the Committee on Religious Liberty.

question remains whether and how far we may also use general principles which would be acceptable to non-Christians and in which they could join us.

There is a tendency of thought which, without refusing in principle this possibility, shows some mistrust and fear that Christians indulge in a too philosophical and 'natural' treatment which could easily become rationalistic or be based on some kind of 'natural law' in the worst style of the Roman Catholic tradition. Others point out the danger that in an interchange with 'secular' thinkers we can only reach what Kierkegaard calls 'agreement on loose concepts', mainly owing to the use by both parties of the same terms but with quite different meanings.

Nevertheless, it would seem that the greater majority of our theologians, while recognizing the reality of the above-indicated dangers and the necessity of avoiding them, believe that Christians may and should find a common field of thinking with non-Christians, and that they can do this in two ways. First, by trying to formulate our Christian convictions (without *mixing* them with the non-Christian ones) in such a manner as to make them as far as possible understandable and acceptable to all men; secondly by accepting the 'natural' reasonings which do not in any way oppose our Christian convictions and which we deem correct in their principles and conclusions. This seems quite possible and would be a sufficient basis for co-operation with non-Christians in an attempt to give positive and universal answers to movements in our own day as, for instance, to totalitarianism in its various forms.

With this spirit and insight, members of the Commission on Religious Liberty developed the following grounds of religious freedom which many outside the Christian Church can also accept, and which we propose to the churches for consideration and discussion.

1. *The dignity and responsibility of man*

Man holds a unique position of dignity and responsibility in his environment. This distinction shows itself in numerous capabilities which equip him for responsibility.

He has a large and increasing dominion over the world of life and matter. The responsible performance of this role demands freedom.

He has unique capacity for personal and cultural growth. The progressive realization of his potentialities calls for freedom to cultivate his mind and to draw on all resources.

He is gifted for and finds satisfaction in creative effort. He needs freedom, including religious freedom, to conceive ideas, project his imagination and formulate his aspirations.

He has capacity for making moral judgments and thereby developing personal character. Enforced conformity is antithetical to the freedom of choice by which he fulfils his responsibility.

He has capacity for voluntary and even sacrificial service. The freedom to respond to the need of one's fellow-man is of highest value to human life and to human relationships.

Moreover, those powers of dominion, growth and creative effort do not exist in isolation. They are aspects of the personality, and they become fully effective only as the personality becomes rooted in an adequate faith. Freedom of access to the sources of faith, freedom of inquiry and discussion, and freedom to profess, exercise and share religious and philosophical insights are therefore essential to human well-being. In isolation man cannot achieve the growth and creativeness which are commensurate with his dignity and responsibility.

2. *Truth and human society*

Persons and institutions who pursue religious ends make a distinctive contribution to man's search for truth when they seek their inspiration without decisive regard for public opinion or for material interests. Cultures and societies need to be informed by moral and spiritual values.

Every man must be free to infuse the culture in which he lives with his own ideas and ideals. This is his opportunity to make his convictions available to other lives and generations. Furthermore, man must be free to associate himself with others in the collective expression of their views. It is not permissible, however, for individuals or groups to force their opinions on others, either directly or indirectly.

Societies which are so closed that they are afraid to provide these freedoms may be motivated by insecurity, by erroneous self-evaluation, or by lack of confidence in unknown patterns. In such situations true human concern, integrity of purpose, and patient communication of thought must underlie every attempt to secure the freedom that is lacking.

3. *Equality and liberty*

Recognition and expression of the fundamental equality of men also requires liberty. Equal opportunity must be afforded to all in the realms of worship, personal development and vocational choice. Discrimination on the basis of social or economic class, racial or national background, family connection or religious heritage, is a curtailment of freedom in matters of religious import.

Such categories as may be created by circumstances or by the human mind must not debase the status of each human being. In the protection of freedom, then, it is important that the concept of equality underlie the theory and practice of jurisprudence.

4. *Liberty and the organized community*

Man's social nature requires for its fulfilment the community experience afforded by social, economic, political and religious institutions. However, man has ends and loyalties which lie beyond himself and his institutions. The recognition of these ends serves to place limits on institutions. Otherwise they are prone to become intractible—the masters rather than the servants of human well-being.

An ordered pluralism of institutions tends to set limits on particular institutions and thereby to ensure to a greater degree the welfare of man. Such pluralism need not lead to social fragmentation nor to conflict. On the contrary, social tension becomes destructive only when institutions aggressively pursue their separate interests.

5. *The concept of justice*

Justice is not limited to constitutional or legal structures; it is concerned with basic principles which societies are not free to transgress. Fundamentally, justice is directed towards the protection of the person and of the conditions of inter-personal relationships. Justice does not protect systems of thought, abstract concepts or even the supposed 'rights of truth'. It protects human beings, however small the minorities they represent or however unpopular the ideas they advocate. It also protects human beings in their material and economic needs, for social and economic justice is an essential condition if humanity is to develop its full spiritual possibilities.

Both constitutional documents and civil law should include adequate guarantees of the rights of persons in society. They must assure adequate freedom for religious and other institutions. In particular, since religious loyalties transcend the loyalties that can be required by law, no participation in an overt religious action should either be required or prohibited by law.

We hope that the above-expressed insights are not alien to the Christian 'ethos' and that, on the other hand, they are acceptable to many non-Christians. We personally think that the Christian concern and the general secular or sociological interest in liberty thus supplement and reinforce each other. Starting from different assumptions they converge towards the same conclusions. Secular thinkers generally believe that society is constantly in the process of adjustment to new developments and changing conditions. The most advantageous adjustments can only be found by giving free play to the imagination, inventiveness, intelligence and industry of persons in every walk of life, so that every idea of possible value will be considered and tested. The source of new values is unpredictable, for no man or group of men possesses the capacity conclusively to determine the potentialities of other human beings. Hence, the maximum freedom for every individual is most conducive to the enrichment of society and indirectly to the well-being of its members. Conversely, the Christian view is that man, the child of God in Christ, is called to freedom. The exercise of free choice and the bearing of responsibility for the results of his choice are essential to the attainment of a mature human stature, and so, indirectly, to the health of society.

Secular thinkers like to underline that religious liberty should also include the freedom *not to believe* or not to have any religious faith.[1] Therefore, we think we should not close our consideration of the philosophical approach without paying attention to such a topic.

Secular opinion is here in harmony with the ecumenical view,

[1] Cf., for instance, the recent article by Robert Bendiner, 'Our Right Not to Believe', *Saturday Evening Post*, 10th February, 1962.

at least concerning the conclusion itself. It seems clear that, for ecumenical agencies, man has not only freedom of positive belief, but also the right not to believe or not to profess any religion at all. This was explicitly declared by the First Evangelical Conference of Latin America,[1] and recently the Third Assembly of the World Council of Churches proclaimed the universal and fundamental right 'to maintain one's belief *or disbelief*'.[2] Within the Commission on Religious Liberty there was general concern that our Christian insights should be objective 'in formulating a doctrine of religious liberty that would equally apply to all persons—to Christians and non-Christians, believers and non-believers alike'. Particularly concerning the freedom not to believe, the Commission was of the unanimous opinion that 'only where there is liberty not to believe can liberty to believe be regarded as free and untrammelled'.[3]

A great majority of our theologians thought that the general Christian insights adduced as foundation for religious liberty perfectly applied to this particular case of freedom not to believe. The status of man, as it appears in the light of the divine revelation, and God's redemptive ways of respecting man's responsible freedom in religious matters, sets humanity in full possession of its liberty to respond, in one way or another, to God's calling, and of not responding at all. There is the risk, accepted by God, of erring by adhering to a false religion, and the similar risk of erring by refusing every religious allegiance.

For some theologians there is also some particular biblical confirmation of this insight in the fact that 'the sun rises on the evil and the good',[4] and in the thought expressed in the parables of the Kingdom: the 'tares'[5] and the 'net'.[6]

---

[1] First Evangelical Conference of Latin America, Buenos Aires, 1949.
[2] Third Assembly of the WCC, New Delhi, 1961, Statement on Religious Liberty.
[3] Minutes of the Meeting of the Commission on Religious Liberty, Spittal, 1959.
[4] Cf. Matt. 5.45.   [5] Cf. Matt. 13.24–30.   [6] Cf. Matt. 13.47–50.

III

HOW RELIGIOUS FREEDOM CAN BE EXERCISED

I

THE RESPONSIBLE EXERCISE OF
RELIGIOUS LIBERTY

IT CANNOT be denied that, as ecumenical agencies see it, religious freedom is not absolute and that it ought to be exercised responsibly.[1]

Nevertheless, we must say that this is precisely the matter concerning religious liberty in which the differences between various churches and Christian groups are most visible and important. Even within each Christian tradition the views are often very distant from one another, and the controversy thereon frequently takes unpleasant forms.

One of the grounds for having different opinions in this matter is *the different factual situations of the churches and religious groups in religious, social and political environment:*

(*a*) There are, for instance, minority churches in countries with other predominant confessions who often suffer grave and unjust limitations in their religious freedom. Obviously these churches and Christians feel very strongly about their need of freedom and are very jealous of securing and defending it. The natural consequence is that in their understandable 'apologetic' complex[2] they do not like to speak of 'responsibility' and of 'limitations' of religious freedom. Even recognizing that freedom cannot be unlimited in principle, they often think that it is not the role of the Church or of the World Council of Churches to make such statements, for the State cares only too well about it. A distinguished professor, now deceased, wrote recently: 'I got the impression that those gentlemen of the ecumenical movement trust very little in liberty. They cannot speak of it without making

---

[1] Cf., for instance, Third Assembly of the WCC, New Delhi, 1961, Report on 'Christian Witness, Proselytism and Religious Liberty'.
[2] See above, Introduction, pp. 11–12.

cool reserves and declaring that freedom must be *responsible* and that it may not interfere with the sacred rights of "morality" and "public order". . . . As if those persecuted on grounds of religion were *ipso facto* suspected of "irresponsibility"! One sees that such definitions of liberty are made by majority churches who enjoy freedom without hindrance but who are always upset when this same freedom is demanded by the "sects". Soon they apprehend the fearful apparition of the ghostly "proselytism" and call to their help the Golden Rule: "Do not proselytize among us, for you do not like our proselytizing among you".' Under the pressure of the hostile official environment it is not rare that they advocate a conception of the State very similar to the concept of the '*État gendarme*' of the liberal individualism, and that they defend a complete separation between Church and State and the most absolute non-competence of the State in matters of religion. Often their 'dualism' or sharp distinction between eternal and temporal things concerns not only the Church–State relationship but in general every social issue and even the individual attitude, so that in these circles one frequently hears 'citizen' and 'Christian' spoken of as two different things which should always be kept separated.

(*b*) Quite different is the opinion of Christian people who live in countries where the State, while recognizing complete religious freedom for all confessions, is favourable to religion in general or even professes concrete Christian principles. For once, they do not see religious freedom in the frame of a 'fighting problem' against the State or society, but as a part of the common good of humanity which the Church and State together should favour and protect. Unbridled religious liberty appears to them not only unwarranted and unjust, but also as one of the greatest dangers to freedom itself. Individuals and churches which enjoy and demand liberty without any care for the general good of the community—so they think—prepare the way for a State which, by force of a natural reaction, will take even the power which does not belong to it and deny the very religious liberty which is legitimate and necessary. Furthermore, they see religious liberty not exclusively in an individualistic sense or in a churchly sense, but as a social faculty whose problems and difficulties should be solved in the social context. In short, they do not put the question as a 'dualism' between the individual and society or between

Church and State, still less as a 'fight' between them, but as the general concern of all, as a common problem to be treated in co-operation and mutual understanding in the interests of all. As for the State, they believe that it may and should be responsible for more than merely peace, public order and welfare, and that it is also responsible for the moral concerns of the whole community. It is, therefore, clear to them that the State is not *entirely* foreign to religious problems, so that on this basis could be grounds for religious liberty.[1]

(*c*) There are also Christians and churches which live in countries whose governments are indifferent and even hostile to religion, and in which the social body as a whole does not react religiously. They generally consider that complete religious freedom is somewhat of a luxury which they cannot afford in such surroundings. For them, claiming freedom of religion in a hostile environment would be useless on the one hand and would probably accentuate hard feelings against Christianity on the other. What matters to them is to give a concrete witness of Christian life and to preach with the evangelical deeds of love and '*diakonia*'. On the other hand, responsible *exercise* means to them, in many cases, responsible *renunciation* of freedoms to which they would in principle have rights. For some of those Christians, even the insistence of the World Council of Churches in claiming and demanding religious liberty for all persons in all countries is inopportune and does not correspond to the real needs of Christianity in those countries. As they say, the first Christian concern should be to love in Christ the concrete society in which Christians live, with all their circumstances and their social and political elements. They not only do not admit any 'dualism', but think that Christians should co-operate with society in any case, even when society or State is contrary to religion. In their opinion, therefore, the social problem of religion should not be put in terms of liberty but in terms of Gospel and in terms of a fertile incorporation of Christians into the society to which they belong.

(*d*) To these groups still another should be added: the group of Christians and churches who live in non-Christian countries, particularly where one concrete non-Christian religion is in the

[1] See above, Part II, ch. 4, 'Frontiers of the State's Competence' studied as Christian foundation of religious liberty.

majority. These young churches, with no old tradition, and who wrestle with the day-to-day problems of living together with a non-Christian majority, see the greatest danger in the 'establishment' of the dominant non-Christian religion and in the State becoming an instrument of domination for that religion. It is therefore not surprising that such churches contemplate a 'secular' State, indifferent to all religions, as the best solution for their concrete problems, so that for them the political and juridical ideal concerning religious liberty is what is called the common submission to common non-discriminating law. They do not even demand some specific protections of religious liberty as such, but simply that civil society gives to all, individuals and institutions, the same fundamental rights, without any discrimination or privilege on grounds of religion.

Considering those different tendencies and opinions, it would indeed be rash impertinence coldly to dismiss as unimportant and purely incidental the tremendous problems posed to Christians by their living among such different circumstances and to impose on all an abstract and disembodied theory. On the contrary, we do think that the problems of exercising religious liberty are above all practical problems in which the impact of worldly realities is of paramount importance.

On the other hand, and however grave be the practical problems posed in each different environment, it would seem that our Christian faith and convictions do not allow us to confuse 'principles' with 'contingencies', or to deduce from concrete difficulties and obstacles the impossibility of striving towards a Christian standard in the exercise of religious freedom. Contingencies and obstacles should be considered and taken into account in their proper measure. But it should also be investigated as to whether there are Christian principles in whose light it would be possible to orientate churches and the faithful towards a Christian solution of the problems and difficulties of each particular situation.

The capital question would therefore be this: Is there, in principle, a general Christian standard for the exercise of religious liberty towards which Christianity should strive as much as circumstances permit?

The response of the great majority of ecumenical theologians is that this Christian standard exists and that it is founded on responsibility. We could perhaps formulate this common opinion as follows:

(a) Religious liberty is a *fundamental* value, but it is not a *supreme* value. Freedom of religion is not a goal in itself but a means to a higher goal: religion as such, or the proper relations between God and man, and even between man and man who is considered the child of God in Christ.

(b) Therefore, while exercising religious freedom, one must take into account the superior values of religion as such. If, by doing this, responsible restrictions of this exercise appear necessary or unavoidable, we ought, as Christians, to accept responsibility and limits in principle and recognize that the exercise of religious liberty 'must constitute a responsible commitment before God towards one's neighbour and towards society'.[1]

(c) Responsible restriction of this exercise does, in fact, appear necessary precisely for Christians who base religious freedom on human responsibility as established by God. It would, indeed, be destructive madness to deny that man's freedom has its counterpart in man's responsibility and that each person and each group has a responsibility towards the rest of society. Responsibility is inherent in the very Christian conception of freedom, for man both creates and achieves his destiny in constant relationship with his neighbour: he is made free by God, not to follow every erratic impulse, but to grow to maturity as a social being aware of the ties to his fellows in the community.

(d) Responsible exercise of freedom is of basic importance for guaranteeing the very survival of liberty. Only a responsible view of liberty can lead to the individual and corporate self-mastery that is required to justify the continuation of external freedom. Inversely, without this sense of responsibility for the well-being of one's fellow-men and of the entire community, some governments, even those who are called democratic in face of irresponsible and undisciplined 'libertinage', will be driven more and more to the use of coercion and to consider coercion as a necessary substitute for responsibility in the use of freedom. Those who were reluctant to speak of 'responsible exercise' did not consider the tremendous truth of this assertion sufficiently: 'Responsible freedom is the only alternative to force'. How many dictatorships and how many forceful denials of true freedom have been the consequence of irresponsibility in the exercise of liberty?

These are Christian principles, general Christian standards of achievement in the exercise of religious freedom. They are recognized by the great majority of theologians, although the

[1] Formulation suggested by Prof. Peyrot, Director of the Legal Office of the Evangelical Churches in Italy.

practical problems of their realization in the different circumstances of time, space and culture may present, in some cases, almost irremovable obstacles.

We now think it useful to return to some of the objections indicated above against the responsible exercise of religious liberty, and to consider them in the light of the exposed principles.

'Why be afraid of complete freedom? Is this not the attitude of the majority churches which enjoy liberty themselves, but wish to limit the liberty of the "sects" and suspect everybody else of "proselytism"?' The weakness of this argument is best shown by turning it on those who used it. Why be afraid of legitimate and necessary limitations of freedom? Is it not the attitude of minority churches which have no social sense of responsibility, which consider State and other churches as potential enemies and enjoy the 'fight' against them? Of course, both arguments are equally *ad hominem* and, therefore, both are equally unrelated to the real issue in question.

It has also been said that the proclamation of limits on religious freedom may be dangerous, for the State might take pretext on them for unduly limiting religious liberty. Although in no way minimizing this danger, and even considering it very important to take proper measures to prevent it, we should not forget that religious liberty itself is much more dangerous, for its risk is not temporal but eternal. In spite of this, God is willing to take this enormous risk, and so do we, by proclaiming and demanding religious liberty. This shows that a consideration of eventual danger should not deter us from recognizing religious liberty or from accepting its legitimate restrictions. Note that this argument of danger is very similar to that which allowed the Roman Catholic Inquisition to burn 'heretics' to avoid the danger of eternal loss. Therefore, if there are necessary and legitimate limitations to religious liberty, these must be recognized and proclaimed. If those limitations are somewhat dangerous, owing, for instance, to the hostile attitude of the State, it is our task to try to limit these dangers by our continuous vigilance, never by concealing the truth.

'Well'—they say—'let the State put necessary limitations to religious liberty. It is perhaps its task. Not the task of the churches. The churches should not speak of any limitation.' Certainly it is not the task of the churches *to put* legal limitations to religious liberty. But it is the task of the Church *to recognize* necessary limitations, and this for two main reasons. First, because the Church has the duty to illuminate society in the whole area of religious liberty; it was recognized by the Commission on Religious Liberty that Christians and churches have here a very concrete obligation toward persons placed in positions of civic responsibility. Secondly, because the Church would lose its authority if, while defending religious liberty and condemning unjust limitations, it does not recognize the legitimate ones, thus giving a bad example of defending its own rights without recognizing the rights of others.[1]

Finally, it should be considered that only a few conditions for the responsible exercise of religious freedom are required by exigences of the common good and may therefore be enforced by law, receiving thus a coercive character. Most of those conditions are of a moral kind and are generally beyond the power of the law to enforce. There is then left the moral self-mastery of individuals and institutions. Just as mastery of the physical world involves acceptance of the facts and laws of nature, so too a creative free action in the social realm presupposes an ordered society. Anarchy is not conducive to freedom. Rebellion does not necessarily lead to freedom; the rebel who breaks with society may be less free than the person who uses the opportunities open to him to remould society from within. Without self-disciplined liberty, fear is widespread lest liberty degenerates into unbridled licence; and hence, the recurrent effort to achieve a well-ordered society by the multiplication of laws and sanctions and the consequent diminution of liberty.

The duties of a responsible exercise of religious freedom concern individuals and institutions as well as society as a whole, and the Church as well as the State. They may also be of a purely moral order or sanctioned by legal provisions. All these aspects of responsibility in the exercise of religious freedom will be the matter of the following chapters.

[1] Cf. Minutes of the Meeting of the Commission on Religious Liberty, Spittal, 1959.

2

RESPONSIBLE FREEDOM AND
MAN'S RELATIONSHIP TO SOCIETY

IN THIS chapter we employ the term 'society' in the general sense of human community. The particular problems of responsible exercise of religious liberty concerning institutions such as the Church and other religious bodies, as well as those concerning the civil society or State, will be treated separately in subsequent chapters.

A. *Responsible man*

'The freedom with which Christ has set us free calls forth responsibility for the rights of others. The civil freedom which we claim in the name of Christ must be freely available for all men to exercise responsibly.'[1]

This statement of the New Delhi Assembly enunciates the general principle and sets the central standard of man's behaviour concerning his responsibility in the exercise of religious liberty.

Man's responsibility to God in the exercise of social religious liberty is generally considered as threefold:

(a) Man is responsible *to his fellow-men* for refraining from exercising his liberty in a manner such as to deny others their rights and liberties.

(b) He is responsible *to society* for doing his duty within it and towards it, including that of sustaining religious liberty for all men.

(c) He is responsible *to the State* as a citizen to further its purposes of welfare, justice and order.

As has been rightly suggested by Dr Nolde,[2] these human standards of responsible exercise of freedom correspond, at least on the level of ideals, to the divine standards of God's non-

[1] Third Assembly of the WCC, New Delhi, 1961, Statement on Religious Liberty.
[2] Dr Frederick O. Nolde, Director of the CCIA.

coercive methods and dealings with men. Such an ideal standard carries with it 'the requirement that religious freedom be responsibly exercised by the individual with a readiness voluntarily to accept limitations in the interest of love and justice.'[1]

Nevertheless, the performance of this ideal standard within human reality demands careful consideration with regard to the measure of man's capacity in realizing this ideal. Man is not God, and we may not forget the biblical teachings about the enslavement of man by sin.[2] Sin, weakness and ignorance explain the fact that the ideal standard of responsible freedom cannot always be reproduced in human experience, and give a clue to the limitations of religious liberty by such action as becomes necessary to protect religious freedom itself against irresponsible behaviour.

Irresponsibility must, then, be prevented by social measures. However, and although admitting that consciences may often act irresponsibly, society should be very cautious in its attitude and never *suspect* people of being irresponsible, still less those who are victims of unjust discrimination.[3] As one of our advisers noted, 'one must put a burden of proof on any external processes that determine that consciences are irresponsible'. Acting otherwise would be establishing *a priori* an unjust legal presumption against the exercise of freedom.

Another very important observation has been made by several theologians concerning the relationship of man to society in the exercise of religious freedom. In virtue of our biblical insights and teachings we, as Christians, cannot expect that society will in any case respect our liberty even if we act responsibly. One thing is the ideal standard of human relations, and another quite different thing are the tensions and persecutions which have been and will be the manifestation of the persecuted Christ in the members of his Body. Of course, it is the duty of Christianity to teach people and all worldly powers that everybody, individuals and institutions, should both exercise responsibly and respect religious freedom. But, while doing this, we should never forget the evangelical predictions that the enemies of the Gospel will grow greater and more powerful until the end of time, thus often crushing the most fundamental rights of religious liberty. The consequence of this

---

[1] Cf. above, p. 82, note 1.
[2] Cf. Bishop Newbigin's observations above, Part II, ch. 3, p. 74.
[3] See above, Part III, ch. 1, p. 102.

insight is that our Christian responsibility will not, in many cases, exclude either the possibility that we shall have *only* that freedom which we take ourselves, even against legal prohibitions and social pressures, or the eventual grave risks of our acting freely. There may be times in which the Christian can have only Paul's paradoxical liberty of 'boldly and freely' opening his mouth—'in chains'.[1]

Related to this insight is the demand made to the Christian, responsibly, but also 'boldly and freely', to proclaim the implications of his religious beliefs for the solution of the ethical, economic, social and political questions which are raised in the modern society.[2]

In virtue of their responsibility, Christians as such have something to say in the name of the Gospel about international peace, about respect for human rights, about the place of the family in society, about the right education of youth, about the relations between capital and labour, and about the basic principles regulating the power of the State, to give only a few examples. This is an essential part of Christian responsibility in the exercise of religious liberty, and such that it should be attentively considered and studied by the churches. Several members of the Commission on Religious Liberty were of the opinion that this problem should be the subject of a particular investigation.[3] For our part, we intend to publish a separate booklet on this topic, which we shall offer for the consideration of the churches.

B. *Responsible society*

One of the main concerns of the Commission on Religious Liberty, in its studies and discussions, has been that of placing freedom of religion, so to say, 'in a social context'.

We live in a social age, and social insights constitute a good part of our mentality or '*Weltanschauung*'. Unfortunately, part of our inherited notions about liberty take their origins from a highly individualistic society in the traditional context of the '*Droits de*

---

[1] Cf. Eph. 6.19 f.: 'I open my mouth, and may boldly and freely make known his hidden purpose, for which I am an ambassador—in chains. Pray that I may speak of it boldly, as it is my duty to speak.'
[2] Cf. First Assembly of the WCC, Amsterdam, 1948, Declaration on Religious Liberty; Third Assembly of the WCC, New Delhi, 1961, Statement on Religious Liberty.
[3] Minutes of the Meeting of the Commission on Religious Liberty, Spittal, 1949, particularly the suggestions made by Prof. Søe.

l'Homme'. The philosophers of the eighteenth century, who made
so frequent a use of the slogan of '*Liberté*', saw society almost as
the poison of man and, therefore, thought of liberty mainly as
a weapon to defend the individual against the 'enemy', collectivism.
We are nowadays far from these philosophical presuppositions.
On the contrary, although very much aware of the dangers of a
collective destruction of personal autonomy and dignity, we
generally see within community the necessary and, in principle,
beneficial human atmosphere and in man an essentially social
being. Consequently, if we do not wish to contradict our own
feelings and convictions, our concept of religious freedom and its
practice must liberate itself from the old liberal individualistic
frame and take into account our social attachment and the whole
'complex' of duties both of the individual and of society which this
attachment implies.

This explains why our Christian claims in favour of religious
liberty as well as our principles regulating its responsible exercise
are not exclusively addressed to the State. The issue of religious
freedom is not an individualistic issue of 'man versus State' but
a primarily social business. Thus we are addressing the whole
human society, individually and collectively, and of course *also*
the State.

It seems to us axiomatic that the existence or non-existence of
religious liberty within a society is of great importance to that
society. Many questions, however, depend upon the understanding we have of the function of religious liberty within the
society. What are the consequences of religious freedom for public
life? Does a Christian view of social structure require that there
be religious liberty?

First of all, we find complete agreement among theologians on
the insight that neither religious freedom itself, nor the responsible
attitude of society in face of it, require man's protection against *all*
external social influences.[1] Everyone recognizes, in general, that
for example religious education of youth within the family, and
even at school in accordance with the parents' wishes, the witnessing and preaching of religions and ideologies, the social *milieu* and
atmosphere, while certainly influencing the religious convictions

---

[1] Cf., for instance, the suggestions submitted to the Commission on Religious
Liberty by Prof. Roger Mehl, Professor at the Protestant Faculty of Theology,
Strasbourg, France; member of the Committee on Religious Liberty.

of the individual, do not, in themselves, constitute a violation of religious liberty and, consequently, irresponsible behaviour in society. Hostile views may say that much Christian ritual, preaching, instruction of the young constitute some 'manipulation' of men's minds and emotions. We are right in recognizing that real dangers exist here, as well as in the problem of church discipline. A carrying out of the mandate in full, namely to put our own house in order, will involve study of what liberty means in these intra-church situations and relationships. The present book cannot take up these questions anew. But it is well to begin at once to mention them, to show to our own people and to others that we recognize the problem and intend to face it constructively.

It is obvious, therefore, that a distinction must be drawn between the social influence which is full of charity and respect for the ultimate freedom of choice, and constraint through inveigling or insidious and degrading seduction. However, it was generally recognized that such a distinction between legitimate forms of social conditioning and forms of restraint which must be condemned may become very difficult in the factual and concrete circumstances of social interrelations.

In spite of this practical difficulty, it would nevertheless be possible to establish a general standard of social behaviour which would correspond to the individual duties of man's responsibility towards society. In a way similar to man's duty to act according to the superior interests of the community, society owes it to man to refrain from every coercion, pressure and seduction which are, in their forms and their results, infra-human or degrading human dignity.

One of the forms of this social coercion and irresponsible social behaviour which occurs, alas, only too frequently, is the discriminating economic and professional pressure practised by groups of a predominant religious confession against other believers. The forms of this social discrimination are in many cases so insidious and its real religious motivations so well concealed that it is practically impossible to prevent it by legal action. Thus we see in some countries that skilled professionals or workers cannot find work and are constrained to emigrate or, what is worse, to practise hypocrisy and pretence.

Several theologians stressed, in this respect, the modern import of *psychological* social conditioning and its particular and debasing dangers.[1] It is, in fact, our basic human liberty, the inner freedom of choice, which is nowadays tremendously menaced. We have seen the emergence of hidden persuaders, employing methods of psychological research to work upon us as potential buyers, voters or converts at subliminal and subconscious levels of perception. Political totalitarianism increasingly engages in brainwashing: it is a technique which breaks down personal identity and reduces a person's individuality and his potentiality for free willed action. But in the Western countries we have 'advertising' and 'public relations' which have increasingly worked behind the scenes in politics, big business, labour and religion to mould opinion and attitudes and to influence buyers of goods, voters in elections and potential religious converts.

A technique which needs close attention is 'motivation research'. It reaches into the emotional structure, the unconscious, the deepest sources of motivation in the individual. The intent of such manipulation may well be innocuous; its by-products may also be a positive boon to the community; but manipulation it remains, none the less. The tendency toward dehumanization of man is evident. Man becomes a statistic, a digit; he loses his identity and the expression of freedom. Hidden persuasion, as well as brainwashing, seeks to manipulate and control man's free will. Indeed, this is a form of personal and corporate imperialism which we have scarcely begun to probe in depth and which can result in the ruin of liberty.

Our efforts, therefore, must be waged against all propagandist stereotyping and over-simplification, unethical journalism, immoral political techniques, thought control threatened by misuse of the media of mass communication or their outright control, overt brainwashing methodology and subtle or naive utilization of slogans which perpetuate caricatures and generate partial truths. Above all, we must educate people to do their own thinking and to have their own volition for themselves in complete freedom of choice. Without this internal capacity of independent decisions, our external liberty would very soon become a ridiculous marionette worked by invisible strings. The virility and integrity of our civilization rests on the acceptance that man, creature of God, is a subject of dignity and respect. Hidden persuasion must

[1] Cf., in particular, the suggestions by Sir Kenneth Grubb.

always be brought to the light, for man has been endowed with intelligence and the capacity to choose, and only by exercising that capacity can man assist our civilization under God.[1]

[1] These considerations, by the way, confirm us in the conviction that we should not call 'external' the social liberty demanded by the ecumenical agencies. Social religious freedom demands not only protection against external social coercion, but protection for external *and* internal activities, as we see in the social danger for freedom of choice, which is certainly *inner* freedom. See above, Part I, ch. 1, p. 16 f.

3

RESPONSIBLE CHURCH

As a preliminary observation let us note that what we shall say
about the duties of the Church (understood in a strict sense)
concerning the responsible exercise of religious liberty may and
should also be applied to all the other similar religious bodies and
groups, even of the non-Christian religions. This is a necessary
consequence of the *universality* of religious freedom as we
Christians see it, for it is not a privilege to be granted to Christians
or to the Christian Church that is denied to others.[1] It is indeed
very important to establish that the Christian Church has no wish
to claim for itself rights and privileges which it would deny to
other religious bodies, to other religions[2] and even to the non-
believers.

In fact, the first main duty of the responsible Church concerning religious liberty is to practise it, to proclaim it and to be its
herald before society. This duty, firmly established by the general
obligation of being true to the biblical and evangelical teachings,
becomes still more imperative through historical considerations.
The churches in their constitutional embodiments have often, in
history, lost sight of the principle of freedom. Again and again
they have reverted to the role of a controlling agency. They have
operated in the realms of restraint and coercion rather than in the
realms of freedom. They have reinforced the legal and social
sanctions of secular society with moral and doctrinal precepts no
less authoritarian in character. It is therefore high time that the
Church renews its concern for freedom, if only to make its proper

[1] First Assembly of the WCC, Amsterdam, 1948, Declaration on Religious
Liberty. We find almost the same terms in: The World Conference on Church,
Community and State, Oxford, 1937, Report on 'The Universal Church and
the World of Nations'.
[2] Cf. the Conference of the Protestant Churches of the Latin European
Countries, Chambon-sur-Lignon, 1958, Resolutions on Religious Liberty.

contribution to the growth of a free world society. This is, doubtless, the sense of the statement made by the New Delhi Assembly:
'It is for the churches in their own life and witness, recognizing
their own past failures in this regard, to play their indispensable
role in promoting the realization of religious liberty for all
men.'[1]

It is, of course, the paramount demand of this general obligation
that the churches themselves *respect* legitimate religious freedom.
As the French Study Group for Religious Liberty suggested, 'the
Church may not exercise any kind of coercion, either physical or
moral, in order to persuade someone to profess something that he
says he does not believe, nor to act against his conscience'.[2] The
Church's witness must be made by the strength of the divine
power given unto Jesus in heaven and in earth, and never by the
force of human power.

As we shall see in the subsequent chapter, in so far as churches
and religious institutions are involved in human affairs in the
juridical sphere, they participate in a system which must utilize,
among other methods, that of coercive power. In the strictly
religious sphere, however, the churches must totally abjure the
use of force. This renunciation of coercion as a means of realizing
their spiritual objectives does not leave them weak and defenceless
before other institutions which are ready to use force. Power has
many expressions beside that of coercion, and some of them are
closely related to the *raison d'être* of the Church. Such expressions
of power, which alone are of spiritual significance for the churches,
must inevitably be neglected if these descend to reliance upon
coercion. Although open to debasement,[3] the power of persuasion,
when prayerfully exercised through proclamation, teaching and
example, is ultimately the only adequate way of communicating
the Gospel in its personal and social significance.

Underlying all expressions of power in its spiritual forms must
be the abiding power of God's love reflected in the lives of
dedicated Christians and in the witness of the Church. It was that
love of God which brought Jesus Christ to serve men and to

[1] Third Assembly of the WCC, New Delhi, 1961, Statement on Religious
Liberty.
[2] Suggestions of the French Study Group to the Commission on Religious
Liberty.
[3] See above, Part III, ch. 2, pp. 112–114.

suffer for them. It was that love which gave the victory of resurrection and bestowed his Spirit upon the Church. In that love the Church must find its freedom and continue to rest its confidence. True to this evangelical spirit of love, Paul did not ask the Church to take any other word for religious purposes than 'the sword of the Spirit, which is the Word of God'.[1] Even the Church's essential task of keeping 'the unity of the Spirit' should be done 'in the bond of peace', 'with all lowliness and meekness, with longsuffering, forbearing one another in love'.[2] As a consequence of these insights, ecumenical agencies have called upon the churches 'to guard against the sin of themselves conniving at repression of churches and religious bodies of a faith and order differing from their own. The ideal of ecumenicity demands that the Church in its various branches shall set an example to the world of toleration for all, and specifically for members of minority Christian communions.'[3] As the Central Committee of the World Council of Churches has said, 'our contribution to the promotion of religious freedom throughout the world requires a continuing critical study of our own practices and such modifications of them as the standard of religious freedom requires'.[4]

This Christian spirit of love includes, of course, the Church's complete renunciation of the use of power by the State in religious matters, above all for subjecting or even eliminating religious minorities. The Oxford Conference proclaimed: 'All churches should renounce the use of the coercive power of the State in matters of religion.'[5] And Amsterdam: 'We oppose any church which seeks to use the power of the State to enforce religious uniformity.'[6]

The Church's responsibility primarily demands that its own liberty be exercised with full respect for the freedom of others

[1] Eph. 6.17. [2] Eph. 4.2–3.
[3] The World Conference on Church, Community and State, Oxford, 1937, Report on 'The Universal Church and the World of Nations'.
[4] Central Committee of the WCC, Toronto, 1950, Report on 'Religious Freedom in Face of Dominant Forces': *Minutes and Reports*, p. 75.
[5] The World Conference on Church, Community and State, Oxford, 1937, Report on 'Church and State'.
[6] First Assembly of the WCC, Amsterdam, 1948, Report on 'The Church and the International Disorder'. Cf. also: Resolution of the Central Committee of the WCC, Chichester, 1949; Conference of the Protestant Churches of the Latin European Countries, Chambon-sur-Lignon, 1958, Resolutions on Religious Liberty.

and of the rights and duties of a well-constituted civil society. The Christian Church should not consider such a situation ideal in which, to give the expression of one of our distinguished advisers, 'religious bodies "mill about" in complete freedom, jostling and pushing one another'.[1] On the contrary, 'the churches are called to show such restraint in their exercise of religious liberty as to avoid the causing of offence and in the fullest possible measure to respect the convictions of other churches'.[2] 'Proselytism', therefore, is not condemned by the churches in virtue of a selfish feeling of self-preservation,[3] but because it is the corruption and caricature of evangelism, and because it implies a denial of the Gospel of love.[4]

This Christian reserve and responsibility in the exercise of religious freedom by no means reduces the Church to the altar and the sacristy, to a maimed Christianity cut off from the real life of mankind on earth, which has no value or usefulness for the problems confronting life and which is unable to illumine the miseries and needs of the world of today with the Gospel. On the contrary, the Church has a social witness and mission. It has a word to say on social and public problems both in its own '*kerygma*' (proclamation) and through the participation of its members in the community structures of society.

But, on the other hand, the Church should never be a 'caesaro-papist' institution, always dabbling in politics, ambitious and mundane, exploiting the eternal values as tools, weapons and keys to satisfy its avidity for temporal power. Such a Church would necessarily try to dominate the power of the State in order to impose their own ideals and prejudices and thus destroy that same liberty of which it was so proud.

Certainly it will be, in many cases, difficult to draw correctly a practical line between legitimate Christian witness and the Church's action concerning social and political relations on the one side and undue ecclesiastical interference in society on the other. We shall try to study this problem when considering the

[1] Cf. the suggestions by Sir Kenneth Grubb to the Commission on Religious Liberty.

[2] Third Assembly of the WCC, New Delhi, 1961, Report on 'Christian Witness, Proselytism and Religious Liberty'.

[3] See above, Part III, ch. 1, p. 102.

[4] As another Commission had been appointed for the particular study of proselytism, our Commission did not investigate this problem and, therefore, it is not either a matter directly treated in this book.

Church-State relationship, although well aware that it cannot be completely solved without taking into account the concrete circumstances involved. Nevertheless we think that there is, as explained above, a clear standard of Christian responsibility which should provide guidance to the Church as a whole and to its leaders and members.

A responsible Church also has a duty to participate in the field of *education*, the importance of which has been stressed by the Commission on Religious Liberty,[1] following in this previous ecumenical statements. The Evanston Assembly, while recognizing that legal provisions and international covenants offer a valuable means to the promotion of religious freedom, consider that law is more often the fruit than the seed of community and that, therefore, to build a strong defence of human rights requires vigorous, broad and persistent educational efforts.[2] This should be an important task for the churches by 'a continuing program of education on religious liberty throughout the world-wide constituency, with particular emphasis upon study at the local or parish level'.[3] Furthermore, the Christian churches and national Christian Councils should not limit themselves to an educational effort among their membership, but should also 'assist in educating the adherents *of all religions*[4] towards a fuller understanding of the nature of religious liberty'.[5] The import of this educational task of the responsible Church is greater when 'ignorance among members of the churches of the issues involved seriously affects the cause of religious liberty'.[6]

The Church's responsibility grows greater and more difficult in face of persecution.

It is more difficult because churches who live under conditions where religious freedom is jeopardized are exposed to especially grave temptations as, for example, the temptation to defend the old political or social order, or the contrary one of leaving the

---

[1] Minutes of the Meeting of the Commission on Religious Liberty, Spittal, 1959.
[2] Second Assembly of the WCC, Evanston, 1954, Report on 'Christians in the Struggle for World Community'.
[3] Central Committee of the WCC, Toronto, 1950, Report on 'Religious Freedom in Face of Dominant Forces': *Minutes and Reports*, p. 79.
[4] Our italics.
[5] Eastern Asia Conference, Bangkok, 1949, Report on 'The Church in Social and Political Life'.
[6] *Ibid.*

world to its fate. But the Church's mission is to proclaim the Gospel under new situations which, while bringing new difficulties, may, under God, also offer new opportunities. Similarly, the Church may not sink back into a self-contained existence, for it is called to proclaim the Lordship of Christ in all realms of life and under all forms of government.[1] This duty of the Church to preach the whole Gospel and to witness fearlessly even in hostile surroundings was thus proclaimed by the Central Committee of the World Council of Churches:

'We urge the churches to bear clear corporate witness to the truth in Christ and their ministers to continue to preach the whole Gospel. We urge all Christians to stand firm in their faith, to uphold Christian principles in practical life and to secure Christian teaching for their children.'[2]

However, some of our advisers pointed out the extreme difficulty of the Church's witness in States of strong atheist and anti-religious domination. It is not fear of persecution but concern for the spiritual welfare of the Christian community which can move some churches in such circumstances to weigh carefully the consequences which could derive from an inflexible attitude in face of the civil society and from the uncompromising proclamation of all Christian insights concerning social and public life. In exceptional cases, churches could legitimately consider that they are not lacking in the fulfilment of their duties if they return to the situation of the early Church, only to preach the true doctrine of faith and strive for a life outside the world of public life. This is a most delicate question, and there is general agreement on the opinion that its practical answer must be left to the responsible churches involved, which, in each case, should decide what witness they will have to bear.[3] Naturally, this does not mean that a Christian group or a church can ever renounce essential witness where silence would be a disavowal of Christian faith. Inversely, 'to the church chiefly involved must be left the ultimate decision as to when it must refuse to submit to such state laws,

[1] Cf. the Message to the Churches by the Executive Committee of the WCC, Feb. 1949.
[2] Central Committee of the WCC, Chichester, 1949, Statements on Religious Liberty: *Minutes and Reports*, p. 15.
[3] Cf., particularly, the suggestions to the Commission on Religious Liberty by Professor Scheuner, member of the late Commission on Religious Liberty and one of our most distinguished advisers.

regulations or administrative actions as will curtail essential activities, and to its individual members to choose when to suffer persecution or even death rather than to disobey God and the dictates of their conscience.'[1]

The responsible Church, even in the midst of persecutions, should continue to ask for the recognition of complete religious freedom. 'The Christian Church'—the Eastern Asia Conference affirmed—'cannot accept anything less than the freedom which allows it to be what it is, namely the body through which the Lord Jesus continually calls men and women from all nations, races and religions into communion with himself. The Church dare not become a static minority; it must be an ever-expanding, dynamic, free and open society.'[2] Non-persecuted churches should, as far as prudence will esteem it expedient, step in wherever the divinely willed religious freedom of man is threatened or denied, and resist every oppression by which States would seek to compel their fellow churches to submit to arbitrary laws and to the service of false gods.[3]

Of course, when making this fearless proclamation churches should also take into consideration the dictates of spiritual prudence. Not only the atheist States but also the newly independent States of Africa and Asia, for instance, would be extremely sensitive to any kind of external critique of their churches which could smack of foreign political hostility. As noted by a distinguished German adviser, 'The newest experience from East Germany shows that it may still be possible for the Christian living within that State to utter criticism, but that it will be difficult and even in some cases obnoxious to bring about utterances from without'.[4]

But this necessary prudence will never stop the churches from standing together with all who, in the struggle for freedom, suffer pain and trial.[5] As the Central Committee of the World Council of Churches has declared, 'in loyalty to the word that sounded forth from Amsterdam we shall "stay together" in the certain

---

[1] Conference on the World Mission of the Church, Madras, 1938.
[2] Eastern Asia Conference, Bangkok, 1949, Report on 'The Church in Social and Political Life'.
[3] Second Assembly of the WCC, Evanston, 1954, Second Report of the Adv. Commission.
[4] Cf. the above-cited suggestions by Prof. Scheuner.
[5] Cf. Second Assembly of the WCC, Evanston, 1954, Resolution on Religious Liberty.

knowledge that Jesus Christ is Lord: "Stand fast therefore in the liberty whereby Christ has made you free".[1]

This 'standing together' as related to religious liberty necessarily includes some kind of Christian 'solidarity' with the persecuted churches and, at least, the silent, sympathetic and prayerful support of the whole of Christianity. It may be that churches adopt different attitudes when confronting the same situations and that they differ on the practical criterion to be followed in each case. This difference of opinion should never allow the churches to condemn one another and certainly never allow one church to join the persecuting State in the blame against another church. On the contrary, 'Whenever a church anywhere has for conscience' sake refused acquiescence in the demands of a State, other churches should recognize the principle that is at stake and render such assistance, spiritual or practical, as may be wise.'[2] Of course, in some cases it may be wise not to render such assistance. But churches ought never to deny their Christian fellowship in front of civil society. Moreover, we personally think that these ecumenical insights should extend themselves across the frontiers of ecumenical membership and embrace without discrimination 'all who bear the Christian name'.[3]

Above all, in times of trouble, the Church's expression of its spiritual force in Christ must be through patient steadfastness. The Church, as well as individual Christians, must be prepared to go beyond this patience and forbearance to the willing acceptance of suffering itself. In the faithful acceptance of these trials in emulation of the Lord Jesus Christ there is untold power. In this context, Sir Kenneth Grubb thinks that a new phenomenon, *the ecumenical community*, supranational in nature, with absolute loyalties of its own, should be studied here. Particularly should it be investigated how the witness and struggle of the ecumenical community differs in kind and depth from that of a single church living in a world where institutions are ordinarily confined within nations. We recognize the importance of this question which we offer to the consideration of the churches.

[1] Central Committee of the WCC, Chichester, 1949, Statements on Religious Liberty.
[2] Conference on the World Mission of the Church, Madras, 1938.
[3] Central Committee of the WCC, Chichester, 1949, Statements on Religious Liberty: *Minutes and Reports*, p. 15.

As we have seen, it is the duty and privilege of the Church to be the champion of religious liberty and to exercise this duty responsibly. In doing so, certainly the Church must remain answerable to God alone. But—rightly notes Bishop Newbigin—'it should normally be part of the service of the Church to help the State in its task of safeguarding and transmitting the highest values which the society is capable of recognizing'.[1] This means that the Church co-operates with the State and, when necessary, criticizes it. This relationship of the Church as such *vis-à-vis* the State, and the corresponding responsibilities of the Church, will be treated in the following chapter.

[1] Cf. Bishop Newbigin's suggestions to the Commission on Religious Liberty.

4

RESPONSIBLE STATE AND THE
CHURCH–STATE RELATIONSHIP

THE 'APOLOGETIC' complex of which we have spoken above[1] makes it seem that some ecumenical statements consider the problem of the State's responsibility concerning religious liberty from a negative point of view. The State appears somewhat as a potential aggressor of freedom of religion *against* which we must defend fundamental rights:

'It is presumptuous for the State to assume that it can grant or deny fundamental rights.'[2]

'The destiny of man and the different social activities . . . constitute an irremovable limit of the State which it cannot with impunity transgress.'[3]

'The nature and destiny of man . . . establish limits beyond which the government cannot with impunity go.'[4]

'The Church knows that man has . . . an indestructible value which the State must not impair. . . .'[5]

'Any tendencies in State . . . depriving man of the possibility of acting responsibly are a denial of God's intention for man. . . .'[6] Etc.

This attitude of defence is, alas, very necessary in face of many States' destructive assaults on religious liberty in various countries. However, it does not solve the complex and intricate problem of the State's competence concerning religious activities.

We already explained how different and even in some cases opposite are the opinions of ecumenical thinkers when it comes to

[1] See above, Introduction, pp. 11–12.
[2] First Assembly of the WCC, Amsterdam, 1948, Report on 'The Church and the International Disorder'.
[3] The World Conference on Church, Community and State, Oxford, 1937, Additional Report on 'Church and State'.
[4] First Assembly of the WCC, Amsterdam, 1948, Declaration on Religious Liberty.
[5] The World Conference on Church, Community and State, *ibid*.
[6] First Assembly of the WCC, Amsterdam, 1948, Report on 'The Church and the Disorder of Society'.

investigating the sphere of action of civil society in religious matters.[1] We shall try to ascertain here the points of general agreement and to offer to the churches, with as much clarity as possible, the questions open to discussion.

The first point unanimously agreed on by ecumenical theologians is that the State (as well as the Church, although differently) is an institution *willed and ordained by God*. Indeed, the concept of the State as 'ordained of God' seems to follow in the tradition of good biblical vocabulary and concept. Nevertheless, we wonder whether theologians have sufficiently faced the issue of relating this concept to such modern political ideas as popular sovereignty, or to man's need for social organization. If this were done, perhaps some needless difficulties in clarifying our concepts of freedom (as, for instance, some wrong ideas of institutionalism) would be removed. 'Even those institutions, for which the use of legal coercion is divinely sanctioned, exist by virtue of the love and power of God.'[2] Scripture teaches us to believe that this realm, in which coercion is used, is also ordained of God for a good purpose.[3] Of course, this insight does by no means lead to the identification or to the confusion of Church and State. Law and Gospel are so different and their respective realms move on such different levels that this confusion will never be possible for Christians. A 'Christocratic-chiliastic' civil society is indeed very far from Christ's teachings about the Kingdom of God.[4] It remains nevertheless true that the State is not exempt from Christ's Lordship, and that civil society is also subjected to God's sovereignty and providence.

Another point of agreement seems to be the State's incompetence concerning the judgment and definition of religious truths. As the French Study Group suggested, 'The State has no power to decide about the truth of a religion'. We would say not only 'power' but ability and competence. Even that catechumen, the Emperor Constantine, although considering himself almost a bishop among bishops and not being so scrupulous about the State's interference in Church affairs, forced Christian bishops to

---

[1] See above, Part III, ch. 1, pp. 101–104.
[2] Draft of 'A Christian Statement on the Nature and Basis of Religious Liberty', submitted to the Central Committee of the WCC, St Andrews, 1960.
[3] Cf. Bishop Newbigin's suggestions to the Commission on Religious Liberty.
[4] Suggestions to the Commission on Religious Liberty by Dr Voigt (East Germany), member of the late Commission on Religious Liberty.

theological unanimity but never dared to impose his own personal views on them. There can be discussions among theologians concerning the extension and content of the State's religious competence. Nobody, however, thinks that this competence can ever reach the realm of dogmatic convictions and theological insights. *A fortiori*, the imposition of an ideology, either explicitly anti-religious or non-religious, is alien to civil society, with such potency and exclusiveness as to crush religion. An institution which is not competent to judge among various religious beliefs is still less competent to decide against all religious convictions.

Finally, we also find there is general consensus on the principle that the State has the duty not only to recognize and respect legitimate religious freedom, but also the positive duty to protect it against the many extra-legal forces which tend to limit or destroy it. The State can and should take impartial measures to ensure conditions under which religious institutions live and grow.[1]

This positive task of the State in protecting religious liberty is more urgent today than ever before, for—as we indicated above[2]— human freedom is affected by such things as modern means of communication, propaganda, and the use of drugs and techniques for the distortion of human personality.

Where theological opinion resolutely divides is on the problem of the State's competence concerning religion in general and religious liberty in particular.

The question has been graphically put by one of our advisers: 'Does the State just hold the ropes for religious liberty or does it have a dynamic function?'[3]

For many, the State should intervene as little as possible in religious matters. Civil society should simply recognize the *social fact* of religion and, in many cases, of religious pluralism. The State's duty concerning this social fact is to guarantee the harmonious exercise of the religious activities of all citizens and institutions as well as it guarantees the rest of their activities. The main

[1] Cf. First Assembly of the WCC, Amsterdam, 1948: Report on 'The Church and the International Disorder'; Third Assembly of the WCC, New Delhi, 1961, Statement on Religious Liberty: 'It is the corresponding obligation of governments and of society to ensure the exercise of these civil rights without discrimination.'

[2] See above, Part III, ch. 2, p. 112 ff.

[3] Cf. the suggestions submitted to the Commission on Religious Liberty by Sir Kenneth Grubb.

reasons given for a State's aloofness concerning religion are these three:

(a) Caesar must not intervene in matters which are God's. The task of the civil authority is to promote the temporal welfare of the people. Eternal interests are outside its own concern. In this respect the only task of the civil authority is to let churches, religious bodies and religious people in general look for these eternal concerns in freedom and to protect peace and public order in the exercise of those religious rights.

(b) In face of the diversity of religious beliefs, the State, if it has to secure freedom, justice and equality for all, should be absolutely impartial to religious matters. This necessary impartiality requires that civil authorities do not take part in religious controversies, nor profess any religious convictions.

(c) The modern State is increasingly becoming a monstrous 'Leviathan' which intervenes more and more every day in all aspects of human life and threatens to crush the initiatives and freedoms of individuals and institutions under its monopolizing power. We as Christians, hence committed to the defence of human dignity and autonomy, should resist this obnoxious tendency and try to save at least religious freedom from the State's rapacity.

Other theologians, on the contrary, like to stress the positive responsibility of the State in matters of religion and religious liberty, and the guidance and help which the Church can give to the State in fulfilling its God-given function.

First of all, they believe they can see their opinion confirmed by the New Testament view of political power. Compare, for instance, Dr Wilder's position on this question:

'Romans 13 (in the light of which passage other references can be best understood) should not be modernized so as to teach that there are two orders, one temporal and one eternal, or one concerned with the natural life and one with the spiritual life of man. It is evident that for Paul the State has a sacral character, is related to God's action at least in the sense of the *orgê* (wrath), and may well be related to the "angels" or cosmic powers which play such a large part in Paul's thought. The State, then, although it belongs to this age, yet has, as we would say, a metaphysical character. As man's nature is not dual, so *there is no easy dual distinction between religion and politics*.[1] The State should therefore serve man's salvation *positively* and not only negatively. Its attitude to a plurality of ways of salvation in the same society will be *positive rather than neutral*, but respect for the transcendent character of human responsibility will inevitably carry with it impartiality.'[2]

[1] Our italics.
[2] '*Eleutheria* in the New Testament and Religious Liberty', *The Ecumenical Review*, vol. XIII, No. 4, July 1961, p. 419.

Concerning this necessary impartiality, the defenders of a positive attitude of the State in religious matters think that being 'impartial' towards the different confessions existing within civil society does not imply being 'neutral', for the State cannot be neutral about religious values. One of our advisers writes:

'I think we delude ourselves if we imagine that there can be, throughout the world, a sort of neutral secular political order of government, which presupposes no religious or ideological faith, which embodies no questionable "values", and which holds the ring in complete freedom for a plurality of religious faiths to compete with one another for the allegiance of man. I think that that is a mirage. And the New Testament gives us no ground to expect it. The New Testament surely makes it quite plain that the coming into history of Him who is the Omega, the End of history, necessarily introduces into history a process of polarisation in which men are compelled to take sides, and in which the issues ultimately narrow down to one issue, total welfare for man in Christ, or in some other name.'[1]

Even the State, according to this opinion, will be compelled within measure 'to take sides'. In fact—they say—when the State is expected to secure the necessary order and freedom within which man can develop as a responsible person, and when it should employ its resources to ensure that human freedom should find growing expression in the service of the neighbour,[2] this means that the State is regarded as the subject of moral obligations. But, if this is so, can the acceptance of moral obligations on the part of the State be wholly severed from any acknowledgment by the State of the religious or ideological faith from which those moral obligations derive? And Bishop Newbigin concludes:

'Ultimately we should have to fall back upon the revelation of God in Jesus Christ for an answer. This makes it impossible, surely, to treat the State as something wholly separated from the issues with which we are concerned in the preaching of the Gospel. If the State is bound to acknowledge moral obligations, it is difficult to deny that it ought also to acknowledge truth in the field of religion.'[3]

Naturally these theologians look with suspicion at formulations

[1] Cf. the suggestions submitted to the Commission on Religious Liberty by Bishop Newbigin.
[2] Cf. The World Conference on Church, Community and State, Oxford, 1937, Additional Report on 'Church and State'.
[3] Suggestions by Bishop Newbigin. We hope to interpret correctly Bishop Newbigin's last phrase not in the sense of competence to decide on dogmatic truths, which is unanimously denied to the State (see above, p. 125), but in the sense of some adhesion to general religious principles.

such as 'peace and public order', 'public order and morality' and the like as designations of the State's area of competence as regards religious liberty. They think first that these are elastic terms and can be stretched a very long way. Moreover, in their opinion, experience seems to show that we can no longer think of a universal moral standard accepted by all decent people, as distinct from any revelation. 'We are more and more bound', says Bishop Newbigin, 'to recognize that moral standards depend upon religious or ideological faith. If a government puts down a religious practice like *sutee*, it does so on grounds which are ultimately religious or ideological. Here, therefore, one religious faith confronts another, and one uses the power of government to stop another. It is impossible to evade the perplexity of this problem simply by saying that such things ought not to be done'.[1]

Finally, the representatives of this tendency do not believe that the menace of the 'Leviathan'[2] should lead us to deny this positive competence of the State. On the contrary, wrongly denying legitimate competence to the civil power would cause dangerous reactions in the opposite direction. Thus Sir Kenneth Grubb writes:

'Religious men can ignore the responsibilities of the State, if they like, and rejoice in their agreeable freedom. If they do, they will find, ere very long, that one or more of several diseases will attack both them and society. The total common fabric will become so torn that it will collapse. *The State will so abuse its power*[3] that everyone will wake up too late, to ask why ever they did not realize that it had so much. Or the Church itself will either fail to find its relation to the common life, or will succumb and become a great but fossilized hierarchy.'[4]

The final conclusion of the defenders of this opinion is that the point at which restraints may rightfully be imposed upon allegedly harmful and disorderly expressions of religion should be worked out by the State, and that the actual criteria should be defined in the course of a continuing dialogue between the civil authorities and those elements in the body politic—church, cult, school, etc.—in which the moral and religious traditions of the society are continually proclaimed and corrected.[5]

[1] Cf. the above-cited suggestions by Bishop Newbigin.
[2] See p. 127 (*c*).   [3] Italics are our emphasis.
[4] Observations made to the Commission on Religious Liberty by Sir Kenneth Grubb.
[5] Cf. Wilder, art. cit., *The Ecumenical Review*, vol. XIII, No. 4, July 1961, pp. 419–20.

As we see, this is a very different position from that which considers that the State must be 'definitely secular', that it should not regard itself as the defender of any particular religious belief and ideology, and that it has to be completely separated from the Church and from any other religious group or body.[1]

In spite of the sharp contrast registered between the two related tendencies, there is, however, a point on which both opinions agree, namely that no final answer should be given on these problems without careful consideration of each concrete situation. The variety of questions posed by the various particular circumstances in each country is so great that, although the essential insights are not changed, their practical stress or emphasis is, however, modified. To mention one of many examples, there are some countries with thousands of years of civilization and tradition behind them, which have already such a high degree of spiritual cohesion that their many institutions always operate in unspoken acknowledgment of the superior claim of the society as a whole. But there are again very young countries and newly independent nations, societies which have no such traditional cohesion, in which a mighty spiritual struggle has to be waged day in day out to keep the centrifugal force of sectional interests from tearing the fabric of society to pieces.[2] Obviously, in this second case, the necessity of the civil authority *taking sides* is felt to be more imperative than in the first one, and it will be only natural that the State in such circumstances looks for a centripetal power which is not sheer physical constraint but which has to be an idea which holds the allegiance of men. The consequence is that, considering the problems of the State's competence in religious matters, we should think historically and dynamically and not limit ourselves to the elaboration of abstract principles. Various different situations are possible, and various different solutions may also be derived from the same Christian insights. This consideration leads us to the study of the Church–State relationship and of its manifold expressions.

[1] Cf., for instance, the opinions of the French and Italian Commissions on Religious Liberty. Prof. Roger Mehl, although defending the view that the State should be 'secular', recognizes, however, that the secular nature of the State should not involve moral neutralism, and that it is often difficult to circumscribe the field in which the State should take ethical decisions.

[2] Cf. Bishop Newbigin's observations to the Commission on Religious Liberty.

The World Conference on Church, Community and State distinguished as follows three main different situations concerning the relations between Church and State:

'(a) In a State which is Christian by profession it is self-evident that the Church should be free to the fullest extent to fulfil its function. It should also be evident that where in such a State there are majority and minority churches the same essential liberty to carry out the Church's function should be enjoyed by minorities as well as by the majority. All churches should renounce the use of the coercive power of the State in matters of religion. Membership in a minority church should not be a reason for denying full civil and political equality.

'(b) In a State which acknowledges a liberal doctrine of rights it is equally evident that the Church, like other associations, should have the liberty which its function requires.

'(c) In countries where the Church finds in the theory and constitution of the State nothing on which to base a claim to right, this does not absolve the Church from its primary duty of witness. This duty must then include a witness against such a denial of fundamental justice. And if the State tries to hinder or suppress such witness, all other churches have the duty of supporting this Church and giving it the utmost succour and relief in their power.'[1]

Since 1937, when this declaration was issued, new situations have developed or old ones have taken new forms and aspects. Churches, therefore, have to face and to find solutions for situations other than those exposed in the Oxford Statement as, for instance, the following.

In countries of predominant Catholic tradition there is frequently the danger of the State becoming involved in the defence of the religious *status quo*. The tendency is here to inhibit the activities of other religious denominations in order to protect the closed system of religious unity. Obviously in such cases it is imperative to demand, at least, equal freedom for all and liberation from discriminatory laws and practices. Thus, as Professor Scheuner suggests, there are in those countries two partners in the necessary discussion: 'First, the State to whom must be directed the demands for modern development in cultural affairs, for recognition of human rights especially for religious freedom. Secondly, it will be necessary to inform the majority church in

[1] The World Conference on Church, Community and State, Oxford, 1937, Report on 'Church and State'.

those regions that its attitude is out of connection with the more modern developments in the Catholic Church as a whole'.[1]

Another new development is that of the newly independent nations with a non-Christian majority, mostly animated by an anti-colonialist and nationalist spirit which also influences their religious attitude. The main obstacle to religious freedom here will lie in the strong desire of the new nations for national and political unity, which could easily result in the opinion that religious unity could be a unifying factor. Professor Scheuner wonders whether, in such circumstances, it might be preferable to concentrate on the fundamental values of religious freedom, and to show from Christian doctrine that Christians are loyal citizens of a State which recognizes religious liberty.[2]

The most difficult situation arises in the countries with an atheist government firmly bound to a politico-ideological doctrine with materialistic and dialectic foundations. Here it will always be difficult to find the right line of expression once a State pretends that it also is bound to the best interest of man, that it also is liberating man for his own free development, that it is naturally recognizing freedom of thought and is limiting only those activities that are directed against the social and political welfare of the population. The whole problem will be the more difficult in that those governments are partly right when they stress that only new satisfactory economic conditions can bring true spiritual freedom to mankind. Perhaps the most necessary and urgent measure to be taken in such situations is to show forth in words and deeds the whole dimension of the Gospel message, and to show that it cannot be limited to worship and faith but essentially implies a social witness and a social service of love in the '*diakonia*'.

We have already said that ecumenical opinion is divided on the question of whether the Church should be separated from the State. It would seem, however, that two extreme opinions are generally rejected, namely the position denying that the Church has the duty to co-operate to a certain extent with the State for the promotion and protection of religious freedom, and the

---

[1] Suggestions addressed by Prof. Scheuner to the Commission on Religious Liberty. On the new general trend of the Roman Catholic Church concerning religious freedom, cf. A. F. Carrillo de Albornoz, *Roman Catholicism and Religious Liberty*, Geneva, World Council of Churches, 1961.

[2] Prof. Scheuner's observations cited above.

diametrically opposed view advocating a co-operation which would be tantamount to subjection to the civic power and the loss of the freedom necessary for the Church's special mission. Many ecumenical theologians seem, nevertheless, to be inclined to accept the possibility of an organic or other special connection with the State, always, of course, with the proviso that this connection should never result in an impairing of the Church's freedom to carry out its distinctive mission.[1]

Many other ecumenical thinkers prefer for the Church that situation in which ecclesiastical institutions are merely, as far as the State is concerned, free associations under the law, subject, as are all other associations and corporations, to non-discriminatory legal provisions recognizing and guaranteeing equal liberty for all.

We present to the churches these different opinions concerning the competence of the State in religious matters and the Church–State relationship, with the hope that continued study and discussion might lead to an ecumenical consensus.

One of our advisers finishes his considerations on this matter as follows:

'I suppose we would all agree that there is no final answer. An approach which over-emphasizes the unconditional aspects of religious freedom ignores the power, place and function of the State. The approach which exalts the latter ignores the spontaneity and ultimacy of the human conscience.'[2]

We should perhaps let the matter rest here. Nevertheless, we venture to wonder whether the distinction between pure religious freedom and the other religious freedoms in the exercise of which other human rights are proposed would not throw some light on this question. In spite of the eventual moral duties of the State it seems to us obvious that pure religious liberty, i.e. the freedom which regards our essential relations with God as distinct from our social activities, should not be interfered with by the civil society. This freedom is what the Assembly of Amsterdam calls 'the right to determine one's own faith and creed', a right which involves both the process whereby a person adheres to a belief and the process whereby he changes his belief; it includes also the right to receive instruction and education and the freedom of

---

[1] World Conference on Church, Community and State, Oxford, *loc. cit.*
[2] Cf. Sir Kenneth Grubb's observations.

access to information. It is also to be noted, as is explained by the same Declaration, that these rights are equally claimed for individual persons and for religious institutions or bodies. It would seem that these rights and freedoms of Christians and of the Church are free from every legal or administrative interference, for the State, in whatever theory, is alien to non-social acts and activities.[1]

On the other hand, as soon as the exercise of religious activities presupposes the exercise of other rights regulated by law and having social impact, the State has the proper function of requiring 'obedience to non-discriminatory laws passed in the interest of public order and well-being'.[2] In this last case, the State does not intervene in these activities because they are specifically religious, but inasmuch as they are social activities and presuppose the exercise of other social rights.

At any rate, the legal limitations of religious freedom ought by no means to be arbitrary, and the State must be subject in this matter to certain conditions which will be studied in the following chapter.

[1] First Assembly of the WCC, Amsterdam, 1948, Declaration on Religious Liberty.
[2] *Ibid.*

5

LEGAL LIMITATIONS OF
RELIGIOUS LIBERTY

'In virtually every country there are constitutional and legal recognitions of the right of religious liberty; but, at the same time, there are in practically all cases limitations on various grounds such as national unity, public order, public safety, public morality and the like, which in some instances militate against essential elements of religious freedom. Frequently violations of religious liberty occur when reasonable limitations are invoked in an arbitrary or discriminatory manner. Some limitations of the exercise of religious freedom must be admitted as legitimate. It is therefore extremely important to study which limitations must be considered as abusive and which must be considered as acceptable.'[1]

These are the terms in which the Central Committee of the World Council of Churches has laid down the problem of the legal limitations of religious liberty. Following its suggestions, we intend to study in this chapter:

(a) Whether some limitations of the exercise of religious freedom should be admitted as necessary and legitimate.
(b) On what principles these legal limitations should be based.
(c) What the appropriate legal guarantees could be in order to avoid reasonable limitations being invoked in an arbitrary or discriminatory manner.

It would seem that there is general ecumenical agreement on the principle that *some* legal limitation of the exercise of religious liberty is legitimate and even necessary. The very theologians who do not like the churches or the World Council of Churches to proclaim such limitations recognize, however, that they must exist. The ecumenical statements thereon are explicit: 'Some

---

[1] Central Committee of the WCC, Nyborg, 1958, Adopted Program for Studies on Religious Liberty: *Minutes and Reports*, pp. 83–86.

limitation of religious liberty is necessary. . . .'[1] 'Liberty is not absolute. . . .'[2] 'The State ought to employ its resources to ensure that human freedom . . . should not be used according to the prompting of natural inclination for self-assertion and irresponsible behaviour.'[3] Besides, we find in many other ecumenical statements concrete information about the criterion and conditions which should regulate such limitations, presupposing, of course, their necessity and legitimacy.[4]

In all these statements and declarations there is implicitly a distinction which we should like to underline, namely between *legal limitations* and *responsible exercise* of religious liberty. The concept of responsible exercise is much larger than that of legal limitations, for it also includes moral rules of responsible behaviour which cannot be enforced by law. We may perhaps say that legal limitations constitute a supplementary guarantee considered necessary owing to the imperfection of human responsibility.

Admitted that there must be some legitimate legal limitations of religious liberty, much more difficult is the problem of knowing *on what principles these legitimate limitations should be based*. With perhaps the sole exception of the great Amsterdam Declaration on Religious Liberty, which we shall study later, all the other ecumenical statements employ general formulations whose vagueness and elastic interpretation has already been noted.[5] For instance:

> Religious freedom is 'subject only to the maintenance of *public order and security*.'[6]
> The practice of religious liberty 'cannot recognize any limitations by legal action other than those which are necessary for the defence of *morals and public order*'.[7]

[1] Assembly of the East Asia Christian Conference (EACC), Kuala Lumpur, Malaya, 1959, Statement on Religious Liberty.
[2] Third Assembly of the WCC, New Delhi, 1961, Report on 'Witness, Proselytism and Religious Liberty'.
[3] The World Conference on Church, Community and State, Oxford, 1937, Additional Report on 'Church and State'.
[4] Cf. particularly: First Assembly of the WCC, Amsterdam, 1948, Declaration on Religious Liberty; First Evangelical Conference of Latin America, Buenos Aires, 1949, Declaration on Religious Liberty; Conference of the Protestant Churches of the Latin European Countries, Chambon-sur-Lignon, 1958, Resolutions on Religious Liberty, etc.
[5] See above, Part III, ch. 4, p. 129.
[6] Federal Council of the Churches of Christ in America, Statement on Religious Liberty, 1944.
[7] First Evangelical Conference of Latin America, Buenos Aires, 1949, Declaration on Religious Liberty.

The criterion for limitations of religious liberty is to be fou... the State's duty 'of *maintaining law and order for the well-being of all*'.[1] Limitations of religious freedom are demanded 'in the interest of *public order, health and morality*'.[2]

For many, these general formulations are not only vague and prone to equivocal interpretation but also frequently dangerous in practice, for many States invoke these very grounds of 'public welfare', etc., for unjust violations of religious freedom, particularly the tense, authoritarian States which are more or less perpetually operating in exceptional conditions of 'war', 'emergency', or the like.[3] In short, the ecumenical expressions reproduced above, used to designate the legitimate limitations of religious liberty, seem to be insufficient to determine what precisely are *reasonable* and *necessary* limitations, and what, on the contrary, would be an abuse and constitute a real and unjust violation of religious liberty. How could we find a general standard and a sure criterion on this matter?

We think that the more precise formulations of the great Amsterdam Declaration could give us a lead for finding a satisfactory solution. As we have repeatedly said, ecumenical statements are not, in themselves, infallible. But in this case we have a Declaration adopted unanimously at Amsterdam, which has been explicitly (and also unanimously) confirmed by the New Delhi Assembly.[4] Therefore, we think that we have here a solid ecumenical foundation, and that we should accept the limitations indicated at Amsterdam and confirmed at New Delhi and try to determine any vagueness they may have. Here are the pertinent Amsterdam statements:

A. *Limits of the liberty of conscience*[5]

'The right to determine one's belief is limited by the right of the

---

[1] Conference of the Protestant Churches of the Latin European Countries, Chambon-sur-Lignon, 1958, Resolutions on Religious Liberty.

[2] Assembly of the East Asia Christian Conference, Kuala Lumpur, 1959, Statement on Religious Liberty.

[3] Cf. the observations to the Commission on Religious Liberty, by Prof. Searle Bates. (Professor at the Union Seminary of N.Y., member of the late Commission on Religious Liberty and well-known author of the fundamental book *Religious Liberty: An Inquiry*, New York, 1945).

[4] Third Assembly of the WCC, New Delhi, 1961, Statement on Religious Liberty: 'We reaffirm the Declaration on Religious Liberty adopted by the World Council of Churches and the International Missionary Council in August-September 1948, and hold to its provisions.'

[5] Our headings.

parents to decide the sources of information to which their children shall have access.'

B. *Limits of the liberty of religious expression*

'Social and political institutions should grant immunity from discrimination and from legal disability on grounds of expressed religious conviction, at least *to the point where recognized community interests are adversely affected*.[1] Freedom of religious expression is limited by the rights of parents to determine the religious point of view to which their children shall be exposed. It is further subject to such limitations, prescribed by law, as are necessary to protect order and welfare, morals and the rights and freedom of others.'[2]

C. *Limits of the liberty of religious association*

'It [the liberty of association for religious purposes] is subject to the same limits imposed on all associations by non-discriminatory laws.'

D. *Limits of corporate religious freedom*

'The community has the right to require obedience to non-discriminatory laws passed in the interest of public order and well-being. In the exercise of its rights, a religious organization must respect the rights of other religious organizations and must safeguard the corporate and individual rights of the entire community.'[3]

The first important observation we have to make about these statements is that in the Amsterdam Declaration the limitations imposed upon various religious freedoms differ according to the different liberties. In fact:

(*a*) The liberty of conscience, or right to determine one's belief, is practically subject to no legal limitation at all.[4] We say so because the right of parents to decide for their minor children, rather than a real limitation of religious liberty, is the recognition of the rightful substitution of the minor child by his parents, as long as he is not yet capable of personally exercising responsible freedom.[5]

(*b*) The liberty of religious expression is subject to such limitations, prescribed by law, as are necessary to protect the rights and freedom of others and the 'recognized community interests'.[6]

[1] Our emphasis.
[2] Note that we speak in this chapter exclusively about *legal* limitations, not about moral ones which should not and cannot be enforced by law. Therefore we omit here the limitations indicated in the Amsterdam Declaration which are of moral order.
[3] First Assembly of the WCC, Amsterdam, 1948, Declaration on Religious Liberty.
[4] See note above. For the reason indicated we omit here the moral limitations of the freedom of conscience.
[5] The question of determining at what age the child is capable of personally exercising responsible freedom is frequently discussed in ecumenical groups. We cannot enter here into this point.
[6] We prefer this formulation to the other of 'order and welfare'.

(c) The liberty of religious association is subject to the same limits imposed on all associations by non-discriminatory laws.[1]

(d) Similarly, the corporate religious freedom is limited by the provisions of non-discriminatory laws passed in the interest of public order and well-being.

We must now ask: Why these differences in limiting the various religious freedoms?

It would seem that the only valid and sound explanation is to be found in the objective differences of the various freedoms themselves. Religious liberty *as such*, i.e. freedom of conscience or freedom in our relations to God, must be protected *absolutely* by the civil society without any limitation whatsoever. This is the freedom referred to in the first place by the Amsterdam Declaration. The other religious freedoms, which in their exercise presuppose the exercise of other, not specifically religious, freedoms within society, may be limited inasmuch as the other human rights involved legitimately depend on the State's ruling.

Nevertheless, as we have said,[2] freedom of religious expression, freedom of religious association and corporate religious liberty should by no means be considered as simply one instance among others of the ordinary liberties of expression, association and corporation. Being mixed freedoms, i.e. presupposing as their essential elements religious liberty and other related freedoms, both elements, both values must contribute to the practical worth of such liberties and to their respect and protection by the civil society.

Can this distinction, if properly understood and applied, not lead us to solve some of the difficulties and controversies which we have encountered all along our study?

Thus, for instance, it would seem that there we find the solution to the apparent contradiction between the general conviction that the State may only *recognize* religious freedom but not *grant* it, and the competence of civil authority to limit some religious liberties. It is generally said, and various ecumenical statements confirm this insight, that the State has not the competence to grant or deny religious liberty but only to recognize it.[3] If this is

[1] More will be said later on non-discrimination.
[2] See above, Part I, ch. 2, p. 25.
[3] Cf. First Assembly of the WCC, Amsterdam, 1948, Report on 'The Church and the International Disorder'; Declaration of the First Evangelical Conference of Latin America, Buenos Aires, 1949.

true, how can we speak of *legitimate* legal limitations of religious liberty? It is, in fact, unanimously accepted by legal specialists that only he has the competence or faculty to limit, i.e. to repeal partially, a right, who has also the competence to promulgate, to establish and to grant it. But, if the State has no competence to grant religious liberty, neither has it competence to take it away, totally or partially. This difficulty follows from the confusion of applying to the mixed religious freedoms, which also participate in the nature of the other human rights involved, the properties to be predicated only of the *pure* religious freedom. Freedom of conscience, or pure religious liberty, cannot be granted or denied by the State and, for the same reason, neither can it be legally limited in any way or by any reason, as the Amsterdam Declaration properly declares. Mixed religious freedoms, however, may be *partially* granted and limited inasmuch as the other human rights involved are subject to the State's competence. In other words, the basis for limiting some religious freedoms is always *external* to the essence of religious freedom itself, for religious freedom is not, in itself, dependent on the civil power. The need for order to secure the common good, which is the supreme reason for limiting rights, never refers to religious liberty as such, but to the elements of the mixed religious freedoms which are *not* the specifically religious ones. Obviously, the degree of the competence which can be attributed to the civil authority will always be proportionate to the degree to which the other human rights involved are rightly considered as more or less fundamental. Thus we see in the Amsterdam Declaration that the limitations imposed to the right of religious expression are less than those imposed to the right of association, for the human right of expression and communication is rightly considered more fundamental than the right of association.

Similarly, the distinction between different religious freedoms which we have found in the Amsterdam Declaration could perhaps help us to clarify the issues of the controversy described above about the competence of the State in religious matters. We do not think that the civil power has anything to say or to decide on religious matters *as such*. What troubles many theologians and sociologists, with good reason, is the fact that, in actual experience, many things happen within society, even crimes, which are performed on grounds of religion, and they are properly concerned that State and society should not be left defenceless each time that goods generally considered as essential in a concrete community are attacked under the pretext of religion. As one of them said, evil-doers should be punished by the State even if they act on grounds of religion. But in our distinction full respect is guaranteed to religious liberty *as such*, while the social exercise of the other human rights involved in many cases is regulated by the supreme social imperative of the welfare of the community.

Finally, this distinction eliminates, in our opinion, many of the prejudices and reserves against the general ecumenical formulations of 'public order', 'public morality', 'common good', etc. Very well aware of the supreme value of religion, one is naturally reluctant to see such principles of limitation applied to religious freedom. This reaction is perfectly justified, for those community goods are worth less than the supreme value of the eternal interests implied in religion. But, in fact, such a criterion of limitation as the consideration of the welfare of the community should not, as a principle, ever be applied to religion itself, or to pure religious liberty or freedom of conscience, but to the other social values implied in the non-religious rights which in many cases are combined with religious activities. Thus, for instance, no consideration of public order or common good should ever be a reason for limiting the right freely to choose one's own belief or religion and the right to be socially and legally protected against discrimination in the exercise of this right. We may be allowed to make a last observation to those who find it difficult to accept that the State could have competence in morality without having also some responsibility in religious matters. In our opinion, the State, in imposing limitations on grounds of public morality, need not have a concrete code of morals, still less profess a particular religious confession. It is enough that it registers the social fact of some general moral convictions and feelings (founded on religious beliefs or not), and that consequently it properly protects this moral patrimony of the civil community.

In conclusion, we venture to say that the proposition that the State has power and competence to limit religious liberty is a false proposition unless it is duly qualified in the sense that it can limit religious liberty inasmuch as this freedom is *not* religious liberty, or no longer *exclusively* religious liberty, but that it involves the exercise of other civil rights which the State has legitimate power to grant and to limit. When the exercise of some particular religious freedom presupposes the exercise of other social rights, the State may limit it for reasons of the recognized competence of the civil power. For instance, it is clear that the right of public meeting and assembly is a civil right which may, in some cases, be regulated and limited by the State. Therefore, the right to hold religious public meetings is not completely independent of the State, and civil authority may regulate it with non-discriminatory provisions.

As the Central Committee of the World Council of Churches observed, reasonable limitations may, by some governments, be invoked in an arbitrary or discriminatory manner.[1] It is, therefore, imperative that we study what the appropriate legal guarantees should be in order that such arbitrary limitations be avoided.

We think that the following conditions for legitimate limitation of the exercise of the various religious freedoms which imply other civil rights are generally accepted by the ecumenical theologians.

First of all, every limitation must be *prescribed and regulated by law* and never be left to arbitrary administrative decision. Sad and repeated experience has shown that religious freedom is most often curbed by administrative *fiat*, and, on the other hand, is best protected where it is adequately defined by legal provision. In particular, police controls are a major source of excessive and arbitrary limitations. As one of our advisers observes, 'in many countries they [the police] are considered in the realm of "public order" somewhat apart from ordinary administration which recognizes bounds of authority and the need for established procedure'.[2]

Secondly, such provisions or limitations must be *equally applicable* to all citizens and to all religious organizations, and *never discriminatory*. Ecumenical statements have frequently denounced discrimination in religious matters:

'The rights of religious freedom . . . shall be recognized and observed for all persons . . . without imposition of disabilities by virtue of legal provision or administrative acts.'[3] 'Social and political institutions

---

[1] See above, p. 135.
[2] Prof. Searle Bates' observations to the Commission on Religious Liberty.
[3] First Assembly of the WCC, Amsterdam, 1948, Declaration on Religious Liberty.

should grant immunity from discrimination and from legal disability on grounds of expressed religious conviction.'[1] Etc.

Religious minorities should, in the opinion of ecumenical agencies, be especially protected against discrimination.

'Membership in a minority church should not be a reason for denying full civil and political equality.'[2] 'It should also be evident that where in such a State [which is Christian by profession] there are majority and minority churches, the same essential liberty to carry out the Church's function should be enjoyed by minorities as well as by the majority.'[3]

In this respect, however, we should note with Dr Nolde that non-discrimination is not sufficient for the enjoying of full religious freedom. As he says, 'In an extreme case the exercise of a human right or an essential manifestation of it may be prohibited or restricted *for all*[4] and, while there is thus no discrimination, there is also no observance of the human rights'.[5] Therefore, our first and primary concern must be to promote respect for and observance of human rights and fundamental freedoms, for a consideration of discrimination by itself may be profitless or may even be dangerous. And Dr Nolde concludes, 'If the rights and freedoms are *for all*, there is no room for discrimination. If we fix our attention solely on discrimination we may wander on a dangerous detour.'[6] Non-discrimination is then a necessary, but not in itself a sufficient condition of religious liberty.

Related to non-discrimination is the condition that limitations of the exercise of religious liberty should not be imposed on grounds of particular confessional grounds. We say *particular confessional* grounds, for we recognize that legitimate limitations motivated by the general moral standards and even the general religious insights of the whole civil community may not be discriminatory. But in a religiously pluralistic society every limitation imposed upon one religious group of the community on particular confessional grounds advantageous to another religious group must necessarily be discriminatory and is therefore to be

---

[1] *Ibid.*
[2] The World Conference on Church, Community and State, Oxford, 1937, Report on 'Church and State'.
[3] *Ibid.*   [4] Our emphasis.
[5] Observations by Dr Nolde (Director of the CCIA) to the Conference of Non-governmental Organizations, Geneva, 1955.
[6] Statement on 'Discrimination in the Exercise of Religious Freedom', at the Conference on Eradication of Discrimination and Prejudice, Geneva, 1955.

avoided by the civil authority. As a consequence of this insight, the civil authority may never deny religious freedom to dissenting minorities on the grounds of preserving certain moral religious unity and the privileges of the religious majority. This is clear discrimination, and the limitation of religious liberty in the endeavour to produce or to maintain religious unity within a society is never justified.

As in many countries '*emergency*' situations are invoked for justifying unjust limitation of religious freedom, it must be made clear that emergency regulations must never make the excuse for limitation of a nature *unrelated* to the emergency itself or of a degree exceeding the gravity of the situation. On the other hand, as Professor Peyrot notes, 'Clear and *present*[1] restrictions on the free manifestation of religious convictions and of their implicit consequences cannot be justified by society as a whole for fear of *eventual* dangers'.[2] Finally, limitations imposed under emergency conditions must be removed as soon as possible, and in any case when the crisis is past.

We think that finally there is ecumenical agreement on the conviction that the juridical and practical application of these principles is not easy, mainly because societies differ greatly and all are constantly changing. It is therefore difficult to define in absolute terms what freedom religious institutions should demand in each case or how this freedom should be enacted and expressed. We must always recall the Christian basis of our concern for liberty and draw from it guidance for word and action. Since our stand on religious liberty must be constantly adapted to the needs of changing times and conditions, we must, therefore, constantly formulate afresh the application of our Christian principles.

[1] Our emphasis.
[2] Observations to the Commission on Religious Liberty by Prof. Peyrot.

CONCLUSION

ON CONTEMPLATING the whole series of questions and issues concerning religious liberty which have arisen during the discussions held and the studies made by the members and advisers of the Commission on Religious Liberty, it seems to us that we could distinguish among them three groups:

insights or groups of insights on which there is practically unanimous ecumenical consensus;

opinions on which there is no complete and unanimous agreement, but which are held by a great majority of the theologians consulted;

issues about which the discussion is definitely open and whose solution finds no opinion that could be recorded as prevalent.

Besides, it would appear that the agreements and differences on the various issues raised are often mutually interlocked and that they show perceptible relationships, thus revealing a coherent line of thought in each of the different tendencies and opinions expressed. We think, therefore, it would be useful if we try to clarify these various forms by considering the whole complex of the problems posed and then to offer them to the churches for consideration and study.

We shall, then, attempt to analyse the issues investigated in this book, successively taking into account the two aspects which we have now indicated.

I. BALANCE OF AGREEMENTS AND DIFFERENCES

A. *Issues on which ecumenical agreement seems to be reached*

If we are not mistaken, the following propositions would be generally accepted by ecumenical thinkers:

1. The kind of religious liberty claimed by ecumenical agencies in their statements is the freedom from coercion in religious matters by legal enactment or by social pressure.[1]

[1] Cf. Third Assembly of the WCC, New Delhi, 1961, Statement on Religious Liberty.

2. This kind of religious liberty is then *social* in the sense that it means liberation from any compulsion on the part of society. It can also be called *external* inasmuch as it demands protection against every coercion coming *ab externo* (from outside), although external social compulsion may attain the internal capacity or freedom of choice through psychological conditioning and the like.

3. It is *not* the Christian liberty or freedom with which Christ has set men free, but it is its 'outward expression'.[1]

4. This kind of religious liberty is *not* a specific *Christian freedom* in every sense. In fact many non-Christians and also the United Nations in their Universal Declaration demand the same freedoms in religious matters that Christians demand, although their motivations are not Christian. Nevertheless, we defend a certain area and extension of the various religious freedoms in virtue of our Christian insights, and, in this sense, our notion of religious liberty is a *Christian notion*.

5. The general ecumenical notion of social religious liberty includes many freedoms which are very different in content and in their form of exercise.[2]

6. These various religious freedoms may be aptly classified as the:

   (*a*) right to determine freely or change one's own faith and creed;

   (*b*) liberty of religious expression;

   (*c*) liberty of religious association; and

   (*d*) corporate and institutional religious freedom.

   The three latter kinds of religious freedoms presuppose, in their exercise, the recognition of other civil rights involved.

7. Religious liberty is a fundamental human right.[3]

8. Religious liberty is interrelated to all other human rights, not only because in many cases it presupposes the exercise of other civil freedoms, but also because the safeguard of human rights generally depends on respect for religious freedom.[4]

---

[1] First Assembly of the WCC, Amsterdam, 1948, Declaration on Religious Liberty.

[2] Cf. the various ecumenical statements, particularly the Declaration on Religious Liberty by the First Assembly of the WCC, Amsterdam, 1948.

[3] Cf. the ecumenical statements related above, pp. 33–36. In the future we shall simply say 'religious liberty', it being well understood that we mean that *social* religious freedom demanded by ecumenical bodies.

[4] See above, pp. 39–40.

In this sense it is correct to say that religious liberty is the foundation and guardian of all human rights.[1]

9. The Christian *notion* of religious liberty by no means includes any element of indifferentism, relativism or syncretism. Christians consider God's revelation as the absolute and unique truth, but demand religious liberty for all, including erring men, in spite of that absoluteness.

10. We hold a distinctive Christian basis for religious liberty.[2]

11. Religious freedom is an implication of the Christian faith.[3]

12. Although religious liberty should not be derived from single scriptural passages dealing specifically with Christian freedom, we discover its foundation in the full meaning and nature of the Gospel.[4]

13. Christians see religious liberty as a consequence of God's creative work, of his redemption of man in Christ and his calling of men into his service.[5]

14. The whole of God's plan in creation, redemption and calling is directed towards making man *responsible* for his own acts and, therefore, freedom.[6]

15. The revelation of God in Jesus Christ requires a free response and, therefore, any other kind of response is incompatible with its intrinsic nature.[7] This free response is compatible with God's judgment and with the teachings of the enslavement of man's will by sin and the mystery of election.[8]

16. The Christian revelation, as contained in Holy Scripture, lays upon every man the basic demand that he should first and foremost obey God, and consequently requires of all others that they should in no way circumscribe this obedience.[9]

17. God's love is given in freedom and calls for a free response.[10] The freedom which God has given in Christ implies a free response to God's love.[11]

[1] Cf. the related ecumenical declarations, p. 40f.
[2] Cf. Third Assembly of the WCC, New Delhi, 1961, Statement on Religious Liberty.
[3] See the related ecumenical statements above, p. 56.   [4] Cf. above, p. 56f.
[5] Cf. Third Assembly of the WCC, New Delhi, 1961, Statement on Religious Liberty.
[6] Cf. above, p. 65f.   [7] Cf. above, p. 66.   [8] Cf. above, pp. 74–75.
[9] Conference of the Protestant Churches of the Latin European Countries, Chambon-sur-Lignon, 1958, Resolutions on Religious Liberty.
[10] Third Assembly of the WCC, New Delhi, 1961, Report on 'Christian Witness, Proselytism and Religious Liberty'.
[11] Third Assembly of the WCC, New Delhi, 1961, Statement on Religious Liberty.

18. The use of coercion in Christian witness betrays:

   (a) lack of confidence in the power of the Holy Spirit;
   (b) lack of respect for the redeemed man; and
   (c) lack of recognition of the true character of the Gospel, which is a message of persuasion.[1]

19. It is presumptuous for the State to assume that it can grant or deny fundamental rights.[2]

20. There are philosophical insights which can lay a correct foundation for religious freedom which is acceptable to Christians. However, this kind of consideration should be kept separate from the specific theological insights, and confusion between Christian and natural reasoning should be carefully avoided.[3]

21. Our Christian insights also demand freedom not to believe or not to profess any religion at all, for this risk is equally implied in man's responsible and free response.[4]

22. The exercise of religious liberty must constitute a *responsible* commitment before God toward one's neighbour and towards society.[5]

23. Individ.als should exercise religious liberty responsibly. However, society should always put a burden on any external processes that determine that consciences are irresponsible.[6]

24. Man's responsible exercise of religious liberty also includes the eventual disobedience to unjust legal provisions as well as the Christian responsibility of expressing in word or deed the implications of belief in social, economic and political matters, both domestic and international.[7]

25. While there are some forms of legitimate social influence on the individuals concerning religion, provided they are full of charity and respect for the ultimate freedom of choice, society ought to abstain from every coercion, pressure or seduction which are, in their form and their results, infra-human or degrading to human dignity.[8] Economic social discrimination

---

[1] See above, p. 72ff.
[2] First Assembly of the WCC, Amsterdam, 1948, Report on 'The Church and the International Disorder'.
[3] Cf. above, pp. 91–94.   [4] See above, pp. 97–98.
[5] Cf. above, pp. 104–105.
[6] See above, the consideration explained, p. 109.
[7] Third Assembly of the WCC, New Delhi, 1961, Statement on Religious Liberty. See above, pp. 109–110.
[8] Cf. above, p. 112.

on religious grounds and psychological social 'conditioning' should be particularly condemned.[1]

26. The Church has the responsible duty to proclaim and to be a herald of religious liberty before society.[2]

27. The Church's witness must be made in the strength of the divine power given to Jesus in heaven and in earth, and never by the force of human power.[3] All churches should renounce the use of the coercive power of the State in matters of religion.[4]

28. The churches are called to show such restraint in their exercise of religious liberty as to avoid the causing of offence and in the fullest possible measure to respect the convictions of other churches.[5] Nevertheless, the churches should never decline to preach the whole Gospel, nor to perform its social witness and mission.[6]

29. The responsible Church also has the duty to assist in educating people on matters of religious liberty.[7]

30. In face of persecution, the churches should:

   (a) bear clear witness to the truth in Christ;
   (b) continue to ask for the recognition of complete religious freedom;
   (c) stand together with all who suffer pain and trial; and
   (d) show their spiritual force in Christ through patient steadfastness and the willing acceptance of suffering.[8]

31. The State is an institution willed and ordained by God. However, it has no power or competence concerning the judgment and definition of religious truths.[9]

32. The State has the duty not only of recognizing and respecting legitimate religious liberty, but also of protecting it against the many extra-legal forces which tend to limit or to destroy it.[10]

33. No final answer should be given on the problems concerning the State's competence in religious matters without careful consideration of each concrete situation.[11]

---

[1] Cf. above, pp. 112–113. [2] Cf. above, p. 115.
[3] Cf. above, p. 116.
[4] The World Conference on Church, Community and State, Oxford, 1937, Report on 'Church and State'.
[5] Third Assembly of the WCC, New Delhi, 1961, Report on 'Christian Witness, Proselytism and Religious Liberty'.
[6] Cf. above, p. 118. [7] Cf. above, p. 119.
[8] Cf. above, pp. 119–123. [9] Cf. above, pp. 125–126.
[10] Cf. above, p. 126. [11] Cf. above, pp. 130 ff.

34. In the task of promoting religious liberty in accordance with the community welfare, the State should not dispense with the co-operation of the Church. It is therefore in no way an attempt to meddle with what does not belong to it, but a simple act of obedience to God when the Church, so far as circumstances allow it, becomes the champion of true human freedom in co-operation with the State and, when necessary, in criticism of its measures.[1]

35. Some legal limitations of the exercise of religious liberty must be admitted as necessary and legitimate.[2]

36. Legal limitations of the exercise of the various religious freedoms should take into account the more or less fundamental exigency of each of those freedoms.[3]

37. There must be appropriate legal guarantee to ensure that reasonable limitations are not invoked in an arbitrary or discriminatory manner.[4] Although it is difficult to determine these guarantees in each different situation, the following seem imperative:

   (*a*) Every limitation must be prescribed and regulated by law and never be left to an arbitrary administrative decision.

   (*b*) Such provisions must be equally applicable to all citizens and to all religious institutions.

   (*c*) Limitations should never be imposed on particular confessional grounds.[5]

   (*d*) Limitations based on emergency situations must be proportionate to the emergency itself and disappear as soon as the crisis is over.[6]

B. *Opinions held by the great majority of the theologians consulted*

It would seem that the following insights, if not accepted by all, are nevertheless received by the majority of ecumenical thinkers:

   1. Between inner Christian freedom and social religious liberty there is a double interrelation inasmuch as:

---

[1] The World Conference on Church, Community and State, Oxford, 1937, Additional Report on 'Church and State'.
[2] Cf. above, p. 135f.   [3] Cf. above, pp. 137–142.
[4] Cf. above, p. 142.   [5] Cf. above, pp. 142–143.
[6] Cf. above, p. 143.

> (*a*) social coercion implies in many cases an assault against inner freedom, and
>
> (*b*) Christian liberty itself presupposes a social context.[1]

2. Religious liberty considered as a whole or including all the various religious freedoms is not equivalent to freedom of conscience. Still less are religious liberty and 'tolerance' equivalent.[2]

3. We may recognize a common concept of social religious liberty in which we concur with non-Christians in spite of the fact that our motivations are specifically Christian.[3]

4. Although the exercise of religious freedom in many cases presupposes other civil rights, religious liberty is not merely the application of the other different civil rights to religious matters but constitutes a specifically different liberty.[4]

5. *Mixed* religious liberties do not participate in their exercise of the absoluteness of *pure* religious freedom, namely that freedom whose exercise does not imply the exercise of other non-religious civil rights.[5]

6. Religious liberty is not only a human right but a social faculty.[6]

7. In social and civil order, the juridical character of religious liberty must be accepted in spite of the fact that Christian freedom as such is based on Grace.[7]

8. Being a distinctive human right, religious freedom is specifically different from other human rights and should be singled out for defence.[8]

9. In investigating the foundations of religious liberty we should particularly insist on our specifically Christian reasons.[9] Similarly, we should guard against the temptation to resort to abstract deduction.[10]

10. Religious liberty being the outward expression of the inner Christian liberty, we demand the first *because* of the latter, in other words, inner Christian liberty implies in itself the exigency of social religious liberty.[11]

11. Inner Christian freedom demands religious liberty because between both there are intimate interrelations.[12]

---

[1] Cf. above, p. 59ff.   [2] Cf. above, p. 22, 89.   [3] Cf. above, p. 19.
[4] Cf. above, p. 36ff.   [5] Cf. above, p. 22ff.   [6] Cf. above, p. 33.
[7] Cf. above, pp. 33–34.   [8] Cf. above, pp. 37–39.
[9] Cf. above, p. 92ff.   [10] Cf. above, p. 57.
[11] Cf. above, pp. 58–62.   [12] Cf. above, pp. 59–62.

12. Religious liberty is demanded by the non-coercive spirit and method of God's revelation.[1]

13. The nature of the act of faith implies religious liberty and demands it in the social context.[2]

14. It is the nature and destiny of man which establish limits on the State in religious matters, and not inversely.[3]

15. Althouth our main arguments must be based on Christian revelation, however, our Christian insights on religious liberty can be correctly confirmed by the philosophical considerations of:

    (*a*) the dignity and responsibility of man;
    (*b*) man's search for truth within society;
    (*c*) the recognition of social equality;
    (*d*) the pluralism of institutions; and
    (*e*) the general concept of justice.[4]

16. The Church has the responsible duty to clarify the tenets concerning the responsible exercise of religious liberty and its necessary limitations.[5]

17. Although it can in some cases imperil religious liberty, some organic or otherwise special connection of the Church with the State is not essentially incompatible with religious freedom.[6]

18. Pure religious liberty should be subjected to no legal limitation. Religious freedom whose exercise presupposes other civil rights may be in some cases regulated by the State.[7]

C. *Issues about which no prevalent opinion can be recorded*

1. What are the relationships between social religious liberty and the dictates of conscience? Can religious liberty be defined as the freedom to follow the dictates of conscience in religious matters?[8]

2. Is inner Christian liberty really and wholly independent from social constraint?[9]

3. Does the biblical Christian freedom presuppose a historical–social context?[10]

---

[1] Cf. above, pp. 72ff.   [2] Cf. above, pp. 77–78.
[3] Cf. above, p. 86ff.   [4] Cf. above, pp. 94–97.
[5] Cf. above, pp. 106–107.   [6] Cf. above, pp. 132–133.
[7] Cf. above, pp. 139–140.   [8] Cf. above, pp. 27–32.
[9] Cf. above, p. 58–63.   [10] Cf. above, pp. 60–62.

4. Is man's creation the main Christian ground of religious liberty?[1]
5. Is the consideration of man as *imago Dei* (God's image) relevant for the foundation of religious liberty?[2]
6. Are the considerations of man as child of God and of the dignity of man relevant for the Christian foundation of religious liberty?[3]
7. To what extent does the existence of coercion for the service of God contradict religious liberty? Inversely, to what extent does God's non-coercive action imply a judgment on the coercive elements of human society?[4]
8. What is the importance and the historical impact of the 'secular' contribution to religious freedom?[5]
9. What is the State's competence in matters of religion?[6]

II. RELATIONSHIP OF AGREEMENTS AND DIFFERENCES ON THE ISSUES RAISED

It would appear that, in spite of many differences of opinion recorded in this study, it should be possible to synthesize them and to group them in two great currents or tendencies of the theological thought.

The first general tendency is that which likes to consider inner Christian freedom as completely independent and separate from social religious liberty or, as they say, freedom within the State. We think that from this first theological position flow all other insights of this tendency. Inner and external freedom are parallel but go in separate ways. Therefore, religious liberty cannot be based on the Christian liberty to which it has no relation. Therefore, while Christian liberty is based on love, social religious freedom is merely based on the limitation of the State's power. For this opinion, this limitation of the State's power is very great indeed. The State cares 'for peace and social order' and consequently is alien to religious concerns. It is only natural that, for the defenders of this theory, the content and extension of religious liberty is all-embracing and that its limitations should be, for them, reduced to a minimum. Even the general formulations of

---

[1] Cf. above, p. 67f.
[2] Cf. above, pp. 68–70.
[3] Cf. above, pp. 70–71.
[4] Cf. above, p. 74ff.
[5] Cf. above, pp. 92–93.
[6] Cf. above, pp. 126–134.

morals and public order appear to them dangerous and suspicious, for they could be arbitrarily employed by hostile governments.

The other quite opposite tendency is equally coherent. For those who think that biblical Christian freedom has a very concrete historical–social context, it is obvious that the freedom in Christ and the social religious liberty, although different, must be intimately related. Inner Christian freedom implies, therefore, the recognition of social freedom. God's ways with men, making them responsible in religious matters, demand social respect for this responsibility. As a natural consequence of these insights, the State is viewed as not completely alien to religion but, on the contrary, responsible, under God, for the spiritual welfare of the community. In virtue of this responsibility, civil society must not interfere with the essential responsible and free relations of man with God, but certainly regulate, with the co-operation of the churches, the social expressions of religion in such a manner that they can be harmoniously exercised in a social context without being obnoxious to the things considered as essential by each civil community.

These are, we think, the two main tendencies among theologians concerning religious liberty. There is, nevertheless, hope that through deeper biblical and theological study and constructive discussion the differences could be narrowed and even dissipated.

Appendix One

MAIN STATEMENTS ON RELIGIOUS LIBERTY

WE ARE not able, owing to their great number and extent, to publish here all ecumenical declarations, statements and resolutions concerning religious liberty. Moreover, they have been frequently examined during our study. For interested readers it may be useful to consult the following studies on such statements:

1. *Discrimination in Religious Rights and Practices: Pertinent Statements by the Commission of the Churches on International Affairs and related ecumenical agencies, from 1937 to 1955.* Submitted by the CCIA, 1955.*
2. *Ecumenical Statements on Religious Liberty:* A Systematic Analysis by Dr A. F. Carrillo de Albornoz, 1959.*
3. Dr A. F. Carrillo de Albornoz, 'Main Principles of Religious Liberty Proclaimed by Ecumenical Bodies', *The Ecumenical Review,* July, 1961, vol. XIII, No. 4, pp. 421–6.

We give here in chronological order, a list of the most important ecumenical statements concerning religious freedom in principle:

1937: World Conference on Church, Community and State, Oxford, England:
> *Report on Church and State.*
> *Additional Report on Church and State.*
> *Report on the Universal Church and the World of Nations.*

1938: Conference on the World Mission of the Church convened by the International Missionary Council, Madras, India:
> *Report on Church and State.*

1948: First Assembly of the World Council of Churches, Amsterdam, The Netherlands:
> *Report on the Church and the International Disorder* (pp. 88–97 of the official *Report* of the First Assembly).
> *Report on the Church and the Disorder of Society* (pp. 74–82 of the official *Report* of the First Assembly).

* Available at the Secretariat for Religious Liberty.

World Council of Churches and the International Missionary
Council at meetings in the Netherlands:
> *Declaration on Religious Liberty* (pp. 97–9 of the official *Report*
> of the First Assembly of the World Council of Churches).

1949: Central Committee of the World Council of Churches,
Chichester, England:
> *Statement and Resolutions on Religious Liberty* (pp. 15–16 of
> the *Minutes and Reports*).

First Evangelical Conference of Latin America, Buenos Aires:
> *Declaration on Religious Liberty.*

Eastern Asia Christian Conference, Bangkok, Thailand:
> *The Church in Social and Political Life.*

1950: Central Committee of the World Council of Churches, Toronto,
Canada:
> *Report on Religious Freedom in Face of Dominant Forces*,
> submitted by the CCIA (*Minutes and Reports*, pp. 72–83).
> *Resolution on Religious Liberty* (*ibid.*, p. 83).

1954: Second Assembly of the World Council of Churches, Evanston,
U.S.A.:
> *Report on The Responsible Society in a World Perspective*
> (pp. 112–26 of the Evanston *Report*).
> *Report on Christians in the Struggle for World Community*
> (pp. 130–44 of the Evanston *Report*).
> *Resolution on Religious Liberty* (p. 149 of the Evanston *Report*).

1958: Conference of the Protestant Churches of the European Latin
Countries, Chambon-sur-Lignon (France):
> *Resolutions on Religious Liberty.*

1959: Assembly of the East Asia Christian Conference, Kuala Lumpur,
Malaya:
> *Statement on Religious Liberty.*

1960: Thirteenth Meeting of the Central Committee of the World
Council of Churches, St Andrews, Scotland:
> *Report of the Commission on Christian Witness, Proselytism and
> Religious Liberty in the Setting of the World Council of Churches*
> (pp. 212–18 of the Minutes and Reports).

1961: Third Assembly of the World Council of Churches, New Delhi:
> *Statement on Religious Liberty* (pp. 159–61 of the *New Delhi
> Report*).

In view of their extreme importance, we reproduce here in their
entirety the texts of the Amsterdam Declaration (1948) and of the
New Delhi Statement (1961):

DECLARATION ON RELIGIOUS LIBERTY
(Amsterdam, 1948)

An essential element in a good international order is freedom of religion. This is an implication of the Christian faith and of the world-wide nature of Christianity. Christians, therefore, view the question of religious freedom as an international problem. They are concerned that religious freedom be everywhere secured. In pleading for this freedom, they do not ask for any privilege to be granted to Christians that is denied to others. While the liberty with which Christ has set men free can neither be given nor destroyed by any government, Christians, because of that inner freedom, are both jealous of its outward expression and solicitous that all men should have freedom in religious life. The nature and destiny of man by virtue of his creation, redemption and calling, and man's activities in family, State and culture establish limits beyond which the government cannot with impunity go. The rights which Christian discipleship demands are such as are good for all men, and no nation has ever suffered by reason of granting such liberties. Accordingly:

> The rights of religious freedom herein declared shall be recognized and observed for all persons without distinction as to race, colour, sex, language, or religion, and without imposition of disabilities by virtue of legal provision or administrative acts.

1. *Every person has the right to determine his own faith and creed.*

The right to determine faith and creed involves both the process whereby a person adheres to a belief and the process whereby he changes his belief. It includes the right to receive instruction and education.

This right becomes meaningful when man has the opportunity of access to information. Religious, social and political institutions have the obligation to permit the mature individual to relate himself to sources of information in such a way as to allow personal religious decision and belief.

The right to determine one's belief is limited by the right of parents to decide sources of information to which their children shall have access. In the process of reaching decisions, everyone ought to take into account his higher self-interests and the implications of his beliefs for the well-being of his fellow-men.

2. *Every person has the right to express his religious beliefs in worship, teaching and practice, and to proclaim the implications of his beliefs for relationships in a social or political community.*

The right of religious expression includes freedom of worship both public and private; freedom to place information at the disposal of others by processes of teaching, preaching and persuasion; and freedom to pursue such activities as are dictated by conscience. It also includes freedom to express implications of belief for society and its government.

This right requires freedom from arbitrary limitation of religious expression in all means of communication, including speech, press, radio, motion pictures and art. Social and political institutions should grant immunity from discrimination and from legal disability on grounds of expressed religious conviction, at least to the point where recognized community interests are adversely affected.

Freedom of religious expression is limited by the rights of parents to determine the religious point of view to which their children shall be exposed. It is further subject to such limitations, prescribed by law, as are necessary to protect order and welfare, morals and the rights and freedoms of others. Each person must recognize the rights of others to express their beliefs and must have respect for authority at all times, even when conscience forces him to take issue with the people who are in authority or with the position they advocate.

3. *Every person has the right to associate with others and to organize with them for religious purposes.*

This right includes freedom to form religious organizations, to seek membership in religious organizations, and to sever relationship with religious organizations.

It requires that the rights of association and organization guaranteed by a community to its members include the right of forming associations for religious purposes.

It is subject to the same limits imposed on all associations by nondiscriminatory laws.

4. *Every religious organization, formed or maintained by action in accordance with the rights of the individual persons, has the right to determine its policies and practices for the accomplishment of its chosen purposes.*

The rights which are claimed for the individual in his exercise of religious liberty become the rights of the religious organization, including the right to determine its faith and creed; to engage in religious worship, both public and private; to teach, educate, preach and persuade; to express implications of belief for society and government.

To these will be added certain corporate rights which derive from the rights of individual persons, such as the right: to determine the form of organization, its government and conditions of membership; to select and train its own officers, leaders and workers; to publish and circulate religious literature; to carry on service and missionary activities at home and abroad; to hold property and to collect funds; to co-operate and to unite with other religious bodies at home and in other lands, including freedom to invite or to send personnel beyond national frontiers and to give or to receive financial assistance; to use such facilities, open to all citizens or associations, as will make possible the accomplishment of religious ends.

In order that these rights may be realized in social experience, the State must grant to religious organizations and their members the same rights which it grants to other organizations, including the right of self-government, of public meeting, of speech, of press and publication, of holding property, of collecting funds, of travel, of ingress and egress, and generally of administering their own affairs.

The community has the right to require obedience to non-discriminatory laws passed in the interest of public order and well-being. In the exercise of its rights, a religious organization must respect the rights of other religious organizations and must safeguard the corporate and individual rights of the entire community.

STATEMENT ON RELIGIOUS LIBERTY
(New Delhi, 1961)

Mankind is threatened by many forces which curtail or deny freedom. There is accordingly urgent need to reinvigorate efforts to ensure that every person has opportunity for the responsible exercise of religious freedom.

Christians see religious liberty as a consequence of God's creative work, of his redemption of man in Christ, and his calling of men into his service. God's redemptive dealing with men is not coercive. Accordingly human attempts by legal enactment or by pressure of social custom to coerce or to eliminate faith are violations of the fundamental ways of God with men. The freedom which God has given in Christ implies a free response to God's love and the responsibility to serve fellow-men at the point of deepest need.

Holding a distinctive Christian basis for religious liberty, we regard this right as fundamental for men everywhere.

We reaffirm the Declaration on Religious Liberty adopted by the World Council of Churches and the International Missionary Council in August–September 1948, and hold to its provisions. We recognize the Universal Declaration of Human Rights, proclaimed by the United Nations in December 1948, as an important instrument in promoting respect for and observance of human rights and fundamental freedoms.

Although freedoms of every kind are interrelated, religious liberty may be considered as a distinctive human right, which all men may exercise no matter what their faith. The article on religious freedom in the Universal Declaration is an acceptable standard, always provided that it be given a comprehensive interpretation.

> Everyone has the right to freedom of thought, conscience and religion; this right includes freedom to change his religion or belief, and freedom, either alone or in community with others and in public or private, to manifest his religion or belief in teaching, practice, worship and observance.

The recognition of the inherent dignity and of the equal and inalienable rights of all members of the human family requires that the general standard here declared should be given explicit expression in every aspect of society. Without seeking to be inclusive, we illustrate as follows:

Freedom of thought, conscience and belief, even considered as inner freedom, requires freedom of access to reliable information.

Freedom to manifest one's religion or belief, in public or in private and alone or in community with others, is essential to the expression of inner freedom.

> It includes freedom to worship according to one's chosen form, in public or in private.
> It includes freedom to teach, whether by formal or informal instruction, as well as preaching with a view to propagating one's faith and persuading others to accept it.
> It includes freedom to practise religion or belief, whether by performance of acts of mercy or by the expression in word or deed of the implications of belief in social, economic and political matters, both domestic and international.
> It includes freedom of observance by following religious customs or by participating in religious rites in the family or in public meeting.

Religious liberty includes freedom to change one's religion or belief without consequent social, economic, and political disabilities. Implicit in this right is the right freely to maintain one's belief or disbelief without external coercion or disability.

The exercise of religious liberty involves other human rights. The Universal Declaration proclaims among others the right to freedom of peaceful assembly and association; the right to freedom of opinion and expression including freedom to seek, receive and impart information and ideas through any media and regardless of frontiers; the prior right of parents to choose the kind of education that shall be given to their children; freedom to participate in choosing the desired form of government and in freely electing officials; and freedom to leave and to return to one's country, and to seek asylum elsewhere.

The freedom with which Christ has set us free calls forth responsibility for the rights of others. The civil freedom which we claim in the name of Christ must be freely available for all men to exercise responsibly. It is the corresponding obligation of governments and of society to ensure the exercise of these civil rights without discrimination. It is for the churches in their own life and witness, recognizing their own past failures in this regard, to play their indispensable role in promoting the realization of religious liberty for all men.

UNIVERSAL DECLARATION OF HUMAN RIGHTS

We also wish to reproduce here those paragraphs and articles of the *Universal Declaration of Human Rights*, adopted by the United Nations, which refer directly to religious liberty:

Second Paragraph of the Preamble

WHEREAS disregard and contempt for human rights have resulted in barbarous acts which have outraged the conscience of mankind, and the advent of a world in which human beings shall enjoy freedom of speech and belief and freedom from fear and want has been proclaimed as the highest aspiration of the common people,

ARTICLE 2 (first para. only)

Everyone is entitled to all the rights and freedoms set forth in this Declaration without distinction of any kind, such as race, colour, sex, language, religion, political or other opinion, national or social origin, property, birth or other status.

ARTICLE 16 (first para. only)

Men and women of full age, without any limitation due to race, nationality or religion, have the right to marry and to found a family. They are entitled to equal rights as to marriage, during marriage and at its dissolution.

ARTICLE 18

EVERYONE HAS THE RIGHT TO FREEDOM OF THOUGHT, CONSCIENCE AND RELIGION; THIS RIGHT INCLUDES FREEDOM TO CHANGE HIS RELIGION OR BELIEF, AND FREEDOM, EITHER ALONE OR IN COMMUNITY WITH OTHERS AND IN PUBLIC OR PRIVATE, TO MANIFEST HIS RELIGION OR BELIEF IN TEACHING, PRACTICE, WORSHIP AND OBSERVANCE.

ARTICLE 26 (second para. only)

2. Education shall be directed to the full development of the human personality and to the strengthening of respect for human rights and

fundamental freedoms. It shall promote understanding, tolerance and friendship among all nations, racial or religious groups, and shall further the activities of the United Nations for the maintenance of peace.

Final paragraph of the Declaration:

Nothing in this Declaration may be interpreted as implying for any State, group or person any right to engage in any activity or to perform any act aimed at the destruction of any of the rights and freedoms set forth herein.

NOTICE ON THE WCC SECRETARIAT FOR RELIGIOUS LIBERTY

WE THINK that it will be helpful for readers who do not have the full background of the World Council of Churches studies and activities in their area to have explanatory information on its Secretariat for Religious Liberty.

The various ecumenical statements on religious liberty, particularly the Amsterdam Declaration, the Toronto Report, the statements of the Evanston Assembly and the Report on Proselytism adopted at St Andrews, produced evidence that the final and intentional goal of the WCC in this matter is a very practical one, namely the promotion of religious liberty in the world of today. The Central Committee at Nyborg, while asking for a study on this matter, recognized that 'the essential aim' was that 'of taking effective steps to promote religious freedom' (*Minutes*, p. 84).

Nevertheless, the WCC has been well aware that, for this Christian promotion to be truly effective, 'a proper balancing of study and action' was necessary (*ibid.*); and that the following should be investigated:

(*a*) the Christian grounds which supply a content to the conception of religious liberty and justify claims on its behalf,

(*b*) the different ideological, religious and political forces which work for or against religious freedom, and

(*c*) the different methods used to advance religious freedom and their respective effectiveness (*ibid.*, p. 84).

The instructions given by the Central Committee concerning these studies are the following:

A. OUTLINING OF THE PROPOSED STUDIES

(a) *Study on the Nature and Basis of Religious Liberty*

(1) The general aim of this study is to reach 'a consensus concerning the theological and ethical reasons why religious freedom

must be defended' (*Minutes* of the Central Committee at Nyborg, p. 84).

(2) The practical purpose of such a study is that 'as an outcome of the new theological-juridical-philosophical study and of the proposed analysis, a new formulation of the position on religious freedom should be sought in order to arrive at a solidly established basis of our Christian attitude and of the main lines of our policy concerning religious liberty' (*ibid.*, p. 86). Here we see the intimate interrelations which these three kinds of study should have in the deliberations of the WCC.

(3) The main elements of this study should be:

'it should ask whether there are specifically theological grounds which supply a content to the conception of religious liberty and justify claims on its behalf and what the nature and limits of such liberty are seen to be in Christian theology;

'special account must be taken of the understanding of religious liberty explicitly or implicitly assumed in the beliefs and structure of non-Christian religions, and in humanist approaches, and exemplified in the practices of their adherents;

'similarly, the view of religious liberty, held or implied in political systems, including Communism, must be examined;

'finally the theory and practice of religious liberty within and between the Christian churches, including (as required by the previous instruction of the Central Committee) the Roman Catholic Church, must be clarified;

'while there is clear need for a theological study, full consideration should also be given to philosophical, juridical and social aspects. In this connection the relation of religious liberty to other human rights and the inter-play of all human rights should be taken into account.'

(*Ibid.*, pp. 84–5.)

(b) *Study of the Trends For or Against Religious Liberty*

(1) *Concerning the Forces Opposing Religious Liberty:*

'Consideration should be given to trends and forces that oppose the exercise of religious freedom at various levels, such as government, church and society; and the interrelationship of these should be explored.'

Two types of counter forces are to be studied:

(§) 'Limitations on various grounds such as national unity, public order, public safety, public morality, and the like, which in some instances militate against essential elements of religious liberty;

(§§) 'the attitudes which dominate in a society or church community such as the desire to maintain national unity or to perpetuate ecclesiastical tradition as well as the desire to defend recently gained independence against foreign influences.

'It would seem that these two types of counter forces are sometimes related to each other. The extent to which one is brought into play in support of the other calls for careful analysis.

'Some limitations of the exercise of religious freedom must be admitted as legitimate. It is therefore extremely important to study which limitations must be considered as abusive and which must be considered as acceptable.' (The last sentence shows once again how intimately the three studies are connected.)

(Central Committee, *ibid.*, p. 85.)

(2) *Concerning the Forces Making for Religious Liberty:*

'The effort to promote religious freedom will become more effective if positive factors bearing upon any situation are known to such extent that they can be utilized. These factors include liberal elements in a religious community which practises discrimination, personal contacts among religious leaders, national pride and the desire not to be open to criticism in the debates of the international community, enlightened self-interest, necessity of union against anti-religious attacks, and the like' (*ibid.*, p. 85).

(c) *Study of the Promoting Methods*

'Many different methods are used to advance religious freedom. A study of these different methods and of their respective effectiveness will help the churches and the World Council of Churches to work out a definite policy for the future' (*ibid.*, p. 84).

'The collection and analysis of information about such actions would be highly important:

(1) to indicate the extensive work and considerable effort already undertaken or under way and to take it into account as a guarantee of continuity;

(2) to identify the instances where efforts were successful and the methods which contributed to success or, on the contrary, where efforts failed and why;

(3) to reveal unanswered needs or the need for continuing action; and

(4) to create all over the world a positive and friendly climate of religious freedom' (*ibid.*, p. 86).

On the basis of these findings an 'effort should be made to identify what lies within the peculiar competence:

'of the World Council of Churches and its organs, and under what general conditions the policy and tactics of the World Council of Churches should be undertaken' (*ibid.*, p. 86).

of the member churches: 'The promotion of religious freedom can never be truly effective if it is pursued solely by centralized agencies of the churches. There is need for a relatively inclusive analysis of the part which could helpfully be played by all branches and agencies of the churches and missions' (*ibid.*, p. 86).

B. METHODS OF WORK

(a) *General Rules:*

(1) 'The study should continue the considerable work already done by the ecumenical bodies: the report on "The Universal Church in the World of Nations" of the World Conference on Churches, Community and State, Oxford, 1937; the Declaration on Religious Liberty of the First Assembly of the World Council of Churches, Amsterdam 1948; the Report on Religious Freedom in Face of Dominant Forces, adopted by the Central Committee of the World Council of Churches, Toronto, 1950; the statements of the Second Assembly of the World Council of Churches, Evanston, 1954; and the Report on Proselytism and Religious Liberty adopted by the Central Committee of the World Council of Churches, Galyatetö, Hungary, 1956, should especially serve as a basis to this study and to the further policy of the WCC in this matter' (*ibid.*, p. 84).

(2) 'The essential aim of taking effective steps to promote religious freedom demands a proper balancing of study and action. Therefore the pursuit of the study should in no sense serve as a substitute for action on current violations of religious liberty. The CCIA will continue its work in this field. But it is to be anticipated that the findings of the study, as they are progressively made available, and without waiting for final results, shall increase the effectiveness of action under the existing structure of responsibility in the WCC, IMC, CCIA and other organs' (*ibid.*, p. 84).

(3) 'The various parts of the study, as they are indicated above, are not to be undertaken in consecutive fashion; to whatever extent is feasible, the objectives of the study should be sought simultaneously and concurrently' (*ibid.*, p. 86).

(b) *Particular Suggestions:*

(1) *Nature and Basis of Religious Liberty.* This study 'should consider:

the relations between the fundamental principles involved, the long-range programme required and the immediate problems demanding ecumenical attention.'

(Executive Committee, London, February 1958; see *Minutes* of the Central Committee, Nyborg, 1958, p. 83.)

(2) *Trends For and Against Religious Freedom:*

(§) '*Analysis and Classification of Data.* It would seem necessary to assemble a comprehensive documentation, to collect the data thus far scattered in the various agencies and to submit them to analysis and classification.

This assembling, analysis and classification of data should include *inter alia:*

clauses concerning religious freedom in existing constitutions, in projected constitutions and in other legislation and jurisprudence;

statements and actions of churches and other religious bodies concerning religious liberty;

reports on violations of religious liberty with an appraisal of their reliability; and

reports on situations where problems of religious freedom have been satisfactorily solved with an appraisal of the methods and ways by which this result has been achieved.

'Special attention should be paid to the location of sources of such information and the procedure whereby sources which are reluctant to provide information, may be induced to co-operate.

'Information received as well as the findings of the work of analysis and classification should be progressively transmitted, after proper consultation, to the agency or agencies best equipped for immediate action.

'The assembling of data should be done without in any

sense detracting from existing responsibilities already undertaken by the CCIA or other agencies' (*ibid.*, p. 85).

(§§) *Asian Concern.* 'The East Asia Christian Conference has also launched a study of Religious Liberty in Asia. Certain special emphases in the EACC plan of study may be specially noted here.

'The EACC survey will include "a survey of the traditional social and communal patterns in the various countries with a view to understanding the relation between religions and traditional social institutions and how far traditional communal life recognizes or limits religious freedom"; and the influence "of the dynamic forces at work" in society, on religious liberty; it will also include "a study on the concept of religious freedom in ancient non-Christian faiths both in their traditional and renascent phases", and in the "various ideologies of modern Asian nationalism". It involves a study of the "basis of co-operation with men of other religions and ideologies in the promotion of religious freedom".'

'The WCC Commission should seek to co-operate with the EACC in this study and make full use of its results' (*ibid.*, p. 84).

(§§§) *Religious Freedom and Institutional Forces*

'Any study of this question ought not to regard religious liberty solely in the light of trends and forces. While agreeing with the fundamental conception of liberty as an essential demand of man's moral nature, have we not to ask other questions? Is not religious liberty in practice often a consequence of the prior existence of massive institutions, the State, the Church, the structures of non-Christian religions and cultures, economic institutions and traditional *mores*? What resides in the ethos and purposes of some of these institutions which either hampers or enlarges the area or the expression of religious liberty?' (*Ibid.*, pp. 85–6.)

(3) *Study of Promoting Methods:*

'The findings of this analysis could then be progressively considered by officers of the WCC, the IMC and the CCIA with a view to assigning or reassigning responsibility and the co-ordination of effort' (*ibid.*, p. 86).

C. ORGANIZATION

(a) *Commission:*

'It is proposed that the study should be under the general auspices of the Division of Studies, that a special Committee of about ten persons be appointed for its supervision and that the General Secretary should be the secretary of that committee. It is understood that the committee is at liberty to propose changes in the above proposals to the Executive Committee for its approval. A research-worker, appointed by the Executive Committee, will give full time to this assignment. The study is to be financed for the time being by special gifts' (*ibid.*, p. 86).

(b) *Consultants:*

'The pursuit of this study should involve continuing consultation with CCIA and IMC as well as with the confessional world organizations' (*ibid.*, p. 84).

The following has been authorized by the Third Assembly of the World Council of Churches at New Delhi, 1961, concerning the organization and work of the Secretariat for Religious Liberty:

'1. That in place of the Commission created by the Central Committee, a Committee for the Secretariat for the Study of Religious Liberty be set up to have responsibility for the general supervision of these studies. This Committee would be represented on the Division of Studies Committee by at least two members. It would report to the Divisional Committee, and through it to the Central Committee.

2. That the above Committee and the Secretary should seek competent specialists to pursue further studies concerning the nature of religious liberty as seen by Christians, and of the grounds on which it must be promoted. This study should have two broad aspects:

   (*a*) An investigation of the biblical basis for concern about religious liberty, with close attention to the extent to which the Bible does or does not give guidance in the terms in which the problem is formulated in the twentieth century.

   (*b*) A study of significant thought concerning religious liberty, Christian and otherwise, which has arisen in various epochs of history.

3. That the Committee and Secretariat arrange for the publication of a brochure or booklet, based principally on studies done by the Commission and Secretary up to this time, for the use

of the churches and regional councils. This publication
should seek to state clearly the issues that have arisen during
the discussions, as well as the points on which significant
agreement has been reached. It should include pertinent
questions and be suitable for use as the basis of discussion
in different parts of the world.

4. That the Committee and Secretariat arrange a series of regional
studies on religious liberty which should be launched in an
effort to study the widely varying circumstances that arise
in different situations: e.g. where a nation is dominated by
the ethos of a majority church or national church; where the
ideology of political groups is such as to affect the understanding and practice of religious liberty; where cultural
factors impede the manifestations of religious liberty; where
the emergence of new social patterns, political régimes,
peoples and nations place the whole issue of religious liberty
in a state of flux; where dominant non-Christian religions
play a significant part in the scene.

It is understood that the taking of action on behalf of the WCC in
concrete situations is principally the responsibility of the CCIA as
heretofore.' (See the *New Delhi Report*, pp. 167–8.)

Appendix Three

PERTINENT QUESTIONS FOR USE AS THE BASIS FOR DISCUSSION

A. *On the concept and nature of religious liberty*

1. What do churches mean exactly by 'religious liberty' when they demand it? Does it mean *external* religious freedom in the sense of liberation from or protection against every form of social coercion coming *ab externo* (i.e. from outside) but which can also interfere with our inner psychological liberty? What should be the appropriate term for such liberty? '*Social* religious freedom'? Is the distinction between *inner* and *external* religious liberty equivocal? Which other terminology could be employed?

2. What do churches mean by '*libertas christiana*', i.e. Christian liberty? Has it a specific 'Reformation' sense? Is the Christian liberty an exclusively *inner* freedom? Is it completely independent from the external world?

3. What are the relations between Christian liberty and social religious liberty? Are their notions entirely different? Or does the freedom in Christ as understood in the New Testament include social elements?

4. Is social religious liberty in any sense a *Christian* freedom? Would a theological definition of social religious liberty be possible? Is our own notion of social religious liberty a *Christian* concept? Are the area and extension of social religious liberty, as we understand them, a consequence of specific Christian insights?

5. Are all religious freedoms demanded by the Christian churches of the same specific kind? Is the distinction between *pure* and *mixed* religious freedoms acceptable? Would it be correct to call 'pure' religious liberty '*inner* freedom'? Would it be correct to call it 'freedom of conscience'? Have *mixed* religious freedoms, or those whose exercise presupposes other human rights, the same absoluteness and unconditional exigency as pure religious freedom, or freedom of conscience?

6. In what sense may we say that religious liberty is a *human right*? Is it always and exclusively a human right? Is the notion of *social*

faculty a different and larger notion than that of civil right? Is religious liberty a 'distinctive' or specifically different human right? Does the concept of religious freedom include different and superior essential elements from those of all other human rights? What is the interplay of religious freedom with other human rights? In what sense may we say that religious liberty is the foundation and guarantee of all human rights? Does this assertion flow exclusively from Christian insights?

B. *On the basis of religious liberty*

1. Are there biblical statements which explicitly proclaim social religious liberty in the sense demanded by ecumenical agencies?
2. Are there at least biblical expressions by which social religious liberty can be theologically justified? Can this be done through a literal hermeneutic of concrete texts? Or does religious liberty appear justified rather by the general spirit and ethos of the whole New Testament?
3. In particular, how far is social religious liberty necessarily implied in the Christian freedom proclaimed by Holy Scripture? Do the relations between the freedom in Christ and social religious freedom justify a conclusive biblical basis for the latter?
4. In what sense may we say that civil or social religious liberty is an implication of the Christian faith, and that it has its deepest foundation in the Gospel?
5. Is social religious liberty the fruit and the consequence of an absolute theological exigency or rather the product of some Christian ethos subjected to historical relativism? Do historical or local circumstances merely influence the concrete application of fundamental standards concerning religious liberty, or do they modify even its essential concept and principles?
6. Does the consideration of God's attitude towards and intention for man, as they are revealed in Scripture, justify the Christian claims for social religious freedom? Does this general consideration correctly imply two different but intimately related aspects, namely:

    (a) the consideration of man's status as it appears in the light of the revelation through the divine creation, redemption and calling;

    (b) the consideration of the non-coercive redemptive dealings of God with man?

7. What is the best proper formulation of the status of man inasmuch as he has been created, redeemed and called by God? What is the most essential biblical element of this aspect concerning religious

liberty? Is it creation and 'recreation' (redemption)? Or is it the human responsible destiny willed by God? Could this aspect be best expressed and clarified through a trinitarian formulation?

8. Would it be correct to say that the central thought of the consideration of the non-coercive dealings of God with man is the free responsibility of man in accepting revelation? How can this insight be correctly understood without falling into some form of semi-Pelagianism and without forgetting the biblical context which includes judgment and the possibility of eternal loss? To what extent does God's non-coercive action imply a judgment on and set a standard for the coercive elements of human society and coercion in the relations of man to man? Would this consideration of the non-coercive dealing of God with man be properly expressed through the formulation 'Faith-Hope-Love'? Can religious liberty be based on free 'faith' in the sense of man's acceptance of the divine revelation? How do Christian obedience and Christian love supply a theological foundation for religious liberty? Is the biblical antithesis between Law and Grace relevant for Christian insights concerning the foundation of religious freedom?

9. Could religious liberty be based on the Christian insights concerning limitations of the political power? Are these limitations, in face of religious activities, expressly indicated by revelation? Do they originate from Christian insights which are different from those of the free responsibility of man? For Christian theology, does the free responsibility of man flow from the limitations of political power or, inversely, is civil society limited in its competence because God has set man free for religious purposes?

10. Discussion of this matter usually indicates that secondary theological considerations must be brought into play. What secondary considerations are necessary to support the basic theological argument and how are they related to it?

11. What are the import and the impact of 'humanistic' or 'secular' arguments in favour of religious liberty? Should we employ such arguments? Is there any hope of, and utility in, finding a common basis for doctrinal and practical understanding with non-Christians on problems of religious liberty and of its foundation? Are there rational grounds for religious liberty on which we can agree with non-Christian minds?

C. *On the responsible exercise of religious liberty*

1. What does the 'responsible' exercise of religious freedom mean? Does responsibility in this exercise merely include respect for the similar rights and freedoms of others? Or does it also demand

social concern for the well-being of the whole community? Does religious liberty essentially presuppose its responsible exercise within community? Do the conditions of this responsibility exclusively depend on the contingent circumstances of each situation? Or do Christian insights set a general standard of behaviour which should always be taken into account when solving particular problems?

2. Is religious liberty an absolute and supreme value? Or is it a means to a higher goal, religion itself, and our supreme commitment towards God and towards our brethren in God? How far is responsibility in its exercise the final social guarantee of the very survival of religious freedom? Has the Church a particular duty to enlighten society about responsibility of the exercise of religious freedom?

3. Does human responsibility originate from the divine standards of God's non-coercive methods and dealings with men? How far can the ideal standard of a voluntary readiness to accept limitations in the interest of love and justice be reproduced in human experience? How far and according to what principles are supplementary social measures necessary? Does responsible exercise always presuppose obedience to civil authorities? Or does it, on the contrary, forebode unavoidable tensions and persecutions?

4. What is the Christian understanding of the function of religious liberty within society? Are we required to protect man against all social influence in matters of religion? What are the legitimate social influences in this respect? What are the obnoxious forms of influencing which are infra-human and degrade human dignity? Are the latter reduced to the strict external coercion, or do they include psychological conditioning of the freedom of choice itself? Is there a general standard or principle for distinguishing legitimate and condemnable forms of social influence?

5. What are the Church's responsible duties concerning religious freedom? Does the Church's essential message include the duty of proclaiming and promoting religious liberty? How far should the Church itself renounce any kind of coercion, either physical or moral? Does this renunciation derive from the characteristic message and task given by God to the Church? Should all churches renounce the use of the coercive power of the State in matters of religion? Why is proselytism condemned by the churches? Where is the line to be drawn between proselytism and due evangelical witnessing? Taken for granted that the Church has a social witness and mission, how can we distinguish between legitimate Christian witness concerning social and political relations and undue

ecclesiastical interference in society which would be tantamount to an infringement of religious liberty? What are the Church's educational tasks concerning religious freedom?

6. Are there particular duties of the Church when faced with persecution? What are the practical frontiers of the duty of preaching the whole Gospel under hostile circumstances? Should the Church, even in the midst of persecution, continue to ask for the recognition of complete religious freedom and to protest against violations thereof? What should be the dictates of spiritual prudence for the churches living under persecuting governments and for the churches abroad? What does the duty of Christian solidarity with the persecuted demand? Should Christian fellowship in face of persecution extend itself over the frontiers of ecumenical membership?

7. What is the responsibility of the Church *vis-à-vis* the State concerning religious liberty? What is the State's competence in matters of religion? May the State decide or intervene in the definition and understanding of dogmatic or theological truths? Should the State include in what is termed 'genuine citizenship' the acceptance or the professing of a dominant religious tradition? May the State impose an anti-religious or non-religious ideology? What is the State's duty of legally recognizing and protecting legitimate religious liberty? How far can the State be 'impartial' in religious matters? Should the State have moral standards? Should it have religious insights? What should be the correct formulation of the area in which the State may interfere in religious activities? 'Public order and morality'? 'General common good and welfare'? Are there Christian insights regulating the Church–State relationship? Do Christian convictions demand separation between Church and State? In what sense? Is a co-operation of Church and State concerning the exercise of religious freedom necessary? How can this co-operation be compatible with the Church's independence and with the fact that suffering and persecution is an integral part of Christian witness as the New Testament portrays it?

8. Legal limitations of religious liberty and responsible exercise thereof, are they equivalent concepts? Or is the concept of responsible exercise larger than that of limitation? What are the reasons for legally limiting religious liberty? On what principles are these reasons based? Are these principles derived from the very essence of religious liberty or from other elements external to it? Are all religious freedoms demanded by ecumenical agencies equally important? Do they demand the same recognition and protection by the State? Why and how far may some religious freedoms be subjected to civil regulations? Is it possible to formulate the

legitimate legal limitations of the different religious freedoms in such a manner that their abusive interpretation can be avoided? Is the temporal common good of the civil community a legitimate ground for limiting religious freedom? What is the exact distinction between temporal and spiritual common good? Should the State also be concerned with the spiritual welfare of the civil community? Can religious unity or uniformity be considered as a civil common good? May governments limit religious liberty on grounds of protecting religious unity? What should be the necessary juridical conditions of a legitimate legal limitation of religious freedom?

INDEX OF NAMES

INDEX OF ORGANIZATIONS

INDEX OF SUBJECTS

Figures in bold type indicate where the matter is more fully treated. 'R.L.' stands for Religious Liberty.